Twayne's United States Authors Series

Sylvia E. Bowman, *Editor*

INDIANA UNIVERSITY

Shirley Jackson

TUSAS 253

Photograph by Laurence Jackson Hyman

Shirley Jackson

SHIRLEY JACKSON

By LENEMAJA FRIEDMAN

Columbus College

TWAYNE PUBLISHERS

A DIVISION OF G. K. HALL & CO., BOSTON

Frontispiece photograph courtesy of Viking Press.

Library of Congress Cataloging in Publication Data

Friedman, Lenemaja.
  Shirley Jackson.

  (Twayne's United States authors series ; TUSAS 253)
  Bibliography: p. 167 - 77.
  Includes index.
  1. Jackson, Shirley, 1919-1965—Criticism and inter-
pretation.
PS3519.A392Z65   818'.5'409   74-31244
ISBN 0-8057-0402-7

For Joanne, Linell,
Kerry, and Sandra

Contents

About the Author

Preface

Acknowledgments

Chronology

1. The Life and Times Of   17

2. The Short Stories   44

3. First Novel: *The Road Through the Wall*   78

4. The Psychological Novels   86

5. Novels of Setting: The House as a Personality   104

6. The Family Chronicles   145

7. Overview   155

   Notes and References   163

   Selected Bibliography   167

   Index   179

About the Author

Lenemaja von Heister Friedman was born in Germany and grew up in the Catskill Mountains of central New York. She attended Syracuse University, and transferred to the University of Washington (Seattle) for her bachelor's degree. She spent four years in a New York advertising agency in Manhattan, taught high school English for seven years, and attended Cornell and State University of New York for a Masters degree. In 1969 she earned her doctorate from Florida State University. At present, she lives in Columbus, Georgia, with her four daughters and is Associate Professor of English Literature at Columbus College.

Professor Friedman writes short stories and reviews books regularly for *Choice* magazine. She has also published a bibliography on Restoration and eighteenth-century theater. Her interest in Shirley Jackson began many years ago when "The Lottery" first appeared, and has continued throughout Miss Jackson's career, culminating with the special study of her works and the writing of this critical study.

Preface

Unfortunately, no biography or critical study of Shirley Jackson exists at present. Although her late husband, Stanley Edgar Hyman, was himself a critic, he made a policy of never reviewing or appraising — publicly — her work. He expressed approval, however, when I informed him (by letter) that I had begun this critical study. As it happened, he died shortly thereafter, and I never had the opportunity to meet him.

As a writer, Miss Jackson has been little understood; and, because people insist upon associating her with witches and demons, her true literary worth becomes obscured. Part of this misunderstanding is the fault of the publicity that surrounded "The Lottery" and the subsequent collection of stories of the same title. She has herself been responsible for part of the myth, for she humorously called herself a witch. She believed that there were many mysteries in life that man has not been able to fathom; and her magic lies in these realms — not in the exploration of witchcraft or in secret glimpses into demonic practices.

When Shirley Jackson died on August 8, 1965, many moving tributes were paid her, but perhaps one of the most meaningful and appropriate in defining her as an artist is the *Newsweek* obituary of August 23, 1965, which says in part: "In her art, as in her life, Shirley Jackson who died last week at 45 was an absolute original. She belonged to no literary movement and was a member of 'no school.' She listened to her own voice, kept her own counsel, isolated herself from all fashionable intellectual and literary currents. She was not an urban, or existential, or 'new' or 'anti-novelist'. She was unique."[1] After studying and analyzing her works, we may be able to pinpoint certain techniques, but the "magic" of the total effect remains elusive. Nevertheless, in order to present a fair estimate of her work, we must examine not only her literary strengths but also her weaknesses and limitations. In sum, I attempt to show not only that Shirley Jackson is an important writer but that she is primarily — despite her seriousness of theme — an entertainer, a born storyteller.

Chapter 1 is an account of the major events of Miss Jackson's life, with emphasis on the influences important to her literary career. Here also is a brief look at her nonfiction writing, most of which has autobiographical overtones and adds, therefore, to our knowledge of Miss Jackson as a person. Chapter 2, a review of her short stories, reveals the variety of her themes, hints at her storytelling abilities, and notes characteristics of her style; special attention is given to "The Lottery." Chapter 3, covering her first novel, *The Road Through the Wall*, indicates the scope of her experimentation with the longer novel form and her success in dealing with characterization. Chapter 4, presenting the psychological novels *Hangsaman* and *The Bird's Nest*, shows that Miss Jackson handles the topics of emotional and mental illness with suspense and sympathy and that she makes believable people out of case histories.

In Chapter 5, exposure to the novels in which the house is an important factor — *The Sundial, The Haunting of Hill House*, and *We Have Always Lived in the Castle* — suggests again that Miss Jackson is a master of suspense and that she is expert at creating unusual mood and atmosphere. Chapter 6, treating *Life Among the Savages* and *Raising Demons*, displays the range of her talents at humorous storytelling. Chapter 7 reviews some of her own rules for writing and, in an overview of her work, summarizes the themes she uses but also shows that her created world is a special one by emphasizing the subjects about which she does *not* write.

LENEMAJA FRIEDMAN

Columbus College

Acknowledgments

First I wish to thank the family (the parents and children) of Shirley Jackson with whom I corresponded, for their help and cooperation; especially her mother, Mrs. Leslie H. Jackson; her daughter, Mrs. Joanne Schnurer; her son, Mr. Laurence Hyman, and her daughter-in-law Mrs. Corinne Hyman; thanks also to Mrs. Phoebe Hyman.

Second, I am grateful for the letters and biographical information received from friends and colleagues of the Hymans: Mrs. Thomas Foster, Mrs. George W. Wheelwright, Mrs. James Gould Cozzens, Mr. and Mrs. Murry Karmiller, Mrs. June Mintz, Mr. and Mrs. Bernard Malamud, Mr. Ralph Ellison, Mr. Howard Nemerov, and Mr. Ben Belitt.

Next I am indebted to the Syracuse University Library for permission to use their materials and to Mrs. Amy S. Doherty, the University Archivist; to Professor Joseph A. Bryant, Chairman of the Department of English; to Professor H. W. Herrington, who taught Shirley Jackson; and to Professor Robert S. Phillips, formerly of Syracuse, for the aid of his chronology and bibliography of Shirley Jackson. I am especially indebted to the Columbus College Library and to the kind services of Mrs. Virginia Lee who assisted in gathering materials; my thanks too, to the staffs of the Bradley Memorial Library, the Bennington Public Library, the Bennington College Library, and the manuscript division of the Library of Congress for the permission to read the Shirley Jackson manuscripts, letters, etc.

I am especially appreciative of the kindnesses shown me on my visit to Bennington College and for the pleasant interviews with Mr. Thomas Brockway, Drs. Oliver and Dorothy Hager, Mrs. Thomas Foster, Mrs. Corinne Hyman, Mr. Ben Belitt, Mrs. John Wohnus, Mr. and Mrs. Lionell Nowak, Mr. Lawrence Powers, Mr. George Fincle, Mrs. Lucien Hanks, Mr. Danny Fager, Mr. and Mrs. Walter Lehrman, and Mrs. Percy Sikoka; also thanks to the David

Aldriches for allowing me to visit the former Hyman home on upper Main Street.

I acknowledge gratitude to Farrar, Straus and Giroux for permitting me to quote from *The Road Through the Wall* (1948), *Hangsaman* (1951), *The Bird's Nest* (1954), *Life Among the Savages* (1953), *Raising Demons* (1957), and *The Sundial* (1958); to the Viking Press for permission to use material from *The Haunting of Hill House* (1959) and *We Have Always Lived in the Castle* (1962); and to the *New York Times* for allowing me to quote from "Talk with Miss Jackson" by Harvey Breit.

Also, I acknowledge gratitude to the Viking Press, Inc. for permission to reprint excerpts from *The Haunting of Hill House*, by Shirley Jackson (copyright © 1959 by Shirley Jackson); and *We Have Always Lived in the Castle* by Shirley Jackson (copyright © 1962 by Shirley Jackson).

Last of all, but certainly not least, I thank Mrs. Rachel Baird for her assistance in typing the manuscript.

Chronology

1919 Shirley Hardie Jackson born December 14 in San Francisco.

1923 Jackson family moves to Burlingame, California.

1930 - Attends Burlingame High School. Begins writing poetry
1933 and short stories.

1933 Family moves to Rochester, New York.

1934 Graduates from Brighton High School, Rochester, ranked in
top quarter of a class of sixty.

1934 - Enrolled in liberal arts program at University of Rochester.
1936 Withdraws from college in June, 1936.

1936 - Spends a year at home, writing a thousand words a day.
1937

1937 Enters Syracuse University; originally a journalism major,
later changes to English and speech.

1938 First undergraduate story, "Janice," published in college
magazine. Appointed fiction editor of campus humor
magazine.

1939 Influenced by Leonard Brown, professor of criticism and
literature. Wins second prize in university poetry contest.
Meets Stanley Edgar Hyman. Founds and edits new literary
magazine, *Spectre*, with Hyman as managing editor.

1940 Graduates from Syracuse in June. Married to Stanley Edgar
Hyman immediately after graduation. Moves to New York
City. Hyman appointed editorial assistant for *The New Re-
public*.

1941 First national publication, "My Life With R. H. Macy," in
The New Republic.

1942 Birth of first child, Laurence.

1943 First of many stories for *The New Yorker*.

1944 "Come Dance With Me in Ireland" chosen for *Best American Short Stories, 1944*.

1945   Moves to North Bennington, Vermont, where Hyman begins teaching at Bennington College. Miss Jackson substitute teacher in creative writing. Birth of daughter Joanne.

1948   First novel, *The Road Through the Wall*. Seven short stories published including "Charles" and "The Lottery." Birth of third child, Sarah.

1949   The collection of stories (second book) *The Lottery, or The Adventures of James Harris*. Hymans move to Westport, Connecticut. Mr. Hyman on staff of *The New Yorker*. "The Lottery" included in *Prize Stories of 1949*.

1950   Six short stories published in various magazines.

1951   *Hangsaman*, second novel and third book. The Hymans move back to Bennington. Birth of son Barry. "The Summer People" chosen for *Best American Short Stories, 1951*.

1952   "The Lottery" adapted for television. Eleven stories published including "Night We All Had Grippe."

1953   *Life Among the Savages*, first family chronicle. "The Lottery" adapted for the stage.

1954   Novel *The Bird's Nest* meets with great acclaim.

1956   *Witchcraft of Salem Village*. Release of *Lizzie*, film version of *The Bird's Nest*. "One Ordinary Day With Peanuts" chosen for *Best American Short Stories, 1956*.

1957   *Raising Demons*, second family chronicle.

1958   *The Sundial* and the one-act play *The Bad Children*.

1959   *The Haunting of Hill House*, dedicated to Leonard Brown.

1961   "Louisa, Please" receives Edgar Allan Poe Award.

1962   *We Have Always Lived in the Castle* on best-seller list; named one of year's "Ten Best Novels" by *Time* magazine.

1963   Successful film adaptation of *The Haunting*. Reviews children's books for *New York Herald Tribune*.

1964   "Birthday Party" selected for *Best American Short Stories, 1964*. Member of teaching staff at Breadloaf Writers' Conference.

1965   Named recipient of Arents Pioneer Medal for Outstanding Achievement, Syracuse University. Illness prevents her attending ceremonies. Dies of heart failure on August 8.

1966   *The Magic of Shirley Jackson*, edited by Stanley Edgar Hyman. The play production of *We Have Always Lived in the Castle* opens on Broadway October 20; closes October 24.

1968   *Come Along With Me,* edited by Stanley Edgar Hyman. Contains Miss Jackson's unfinished novel, sixteen short stories, and three lectures.

CHAPTER 1

The Life and Times Of

I *Family*

IN San Francisco on December 14, 1919, Shirley Jackson made her way into a world that was not so frightening as the one she later pictured in her short stories and her novels. The surroundings were friendly, and her family enjoyed comfortable circumstances. Her father, Leslie H. Jackson, born in England, had arrived in San Francisco at the age of fourteen. When his daughter was born, he was employed by the Traung Label and Lithographing Company. Her mother, the former Geraldine Bugbee, came from a family of renowned professional men. The first of these ancestors to settle in San Francisco had been Samuel Bugbee, Miss Jackson's great-great-grandfather, who had arrived in the city in 1854, and had begun a long and successful career as an architect, planning many of the oldest homes, including the Stanford, the Crocker,and the Colton mansions on Nob Hill, and the Grand Opera House.

Samuel's son (Miss Jackson's great-grandfather) John S. Bugbee received his schooling at Harvard and returned to San Francisco in 1862 to pratice law. Once settled, he sent for his sweetheart in Rhode Island, Anna Maxwell Greene — a descendant of the Nathaniel Greene family. Anna's ship arrived by way of Cape Horn; when it entered San Francisco harbor, John came aboard; and he and Anna were married by a Unitarian minister, the Reverend Stebbin, under whose care Anna had made the trip. Some time later, President Benjamin Harrison appointed John as a United States District Judge for Alaska. Their son Maxwell G. Bugbee, who followed in his grandfather's footsteps, became a well-known architect; he married Evangeline Field of the Connecticut Fields, and they had two children: a son, Clifford, and Geraldine (Shirley's mother).[1] Considering the family penchant for architecture, it is not surprising that Shirley Jackson was also fascinated by old houses and that houses play an important role in her fiction.

17

II   *The Early Years*

Two years after Shirley's birth, she acquired a brother, Barry; and then two years later in 1923 the family moved from San Francisco to the town of Burlingame, California, about thirty miles away. Many family men, anxious to enjoy the advantages of suburbia, were forced to accept the disadvantages of commuting daily to the city; such was Mr. Jackson's case. The Burlingame environment in which young Shirley grew up became the locale of her first novel, *The Road Through the Wall,* her only novel to have a California setting.

According to her mother, Shirley began to compose verse almost as soon as she could write. An active child, she was interested in sports, music, literature, and, as she grew old enough, boys. When she was twelve, she won a prize for her poem "The Pine Tree" in a contest sponsored by the *Junior Home Magazine;* she was overjoyed by the news until she learned that the reward was only an additional six months' subscription to the magazine.[2] Later, when she attended the Burlingame High School, she began to keep a diary. Her first entries occur in 1932 when she was thirteen years old and are a record of her many interests. She had been studying the piano, and she refers to the piano duets with which she and her friend Dorothy Ayling amused themselves. The piano was to be a source of pleasure throughout her life; she would spend many hours later with her own family crowded about the piano, everyone singing. She played the violin in the school orchestra, but apparently that instrument did not please her, for she practiced little and then turned to other diversions. She was something of a tomboy, for she records a skate-hockey game in which she and Dot played against four boys. Then there were tennis matches and a day the diary states: "Took bicycles thru the creek today. *Dot's* idea."[3]

Although Shirley seems to have enjoyed her studies, she sometimes had a casual attitude toward homework. One entry notes: "Flunked History today — Ethel and I are both poor guessers!" At the same time, and by way of explanation, she records that she has been spending evenings writing: "Wrote all evening. There was something in my pen, tonight — I thought I'd never be able to write again, after I lost Bud [a young love], but I have noticed even an improvement, I can find nicer words too, they were all in my pen!"[4] Two days later she writes: "Got an idea for a new story"; and then, on February 11, "Pen worked overtime tonight again. Did lots of copying. I'm gonna hire a secretary."

She admits that she enjoyed friends and had a "good time in

Latin, History, Trig and English"; that there were interesting people at school; but that the weekends were a disappointment. "Weekends are awful things — nothing ever happens," she says in another entry. She had, it seems, prepared herself a list of resolutions that indicate what she wanted to be at the start of 1933. Several of these items are significant in that they suggest conditions that continued to remain in the "wish" stage for the rest of her life: for example, she hoped to make herself healthier, but by this she meant "thin," a word she added in parentheses. The fear of being fat and unattractive pursued her for as long as she lived, and it may have been the source of a certain shyness and a sense of inferiority.

She expresses the hope that she will lose this sense of inferiority, that she must cultivate charm, that she would like to be popular. She indicates also that she must cure herself of "wanting to spend so much money," another trait that seems to have remained with her throughout the years, but that marked her later as a generous and gracious hostess. Of the stipulations she makes for herself, perhaps the most noteworthy is the last on the list, which directs that she must "seek out the good in others, rather than explore for the evil."[5] Whether she made a practice of searching out the evil in her personal relationships is difficult to say; however, as a writer, she continued her search for the evil in society and exposed it wherever she found it.

Her habit of regarding days as either lucky or unlucky is reflected in the pages of the diary and seems to indicate her increasing interest in superstition and the supernatural. Her 1932 entries include some that say simply, "Luck," "Luck in the morning," "No luck," or "Luck — all day." Three years later on February 10, 1935, her attitude toward fortune is much the same when she says: "February seems so far to have been a month of evil omen and disillusion."

There were to be big changes ahead, for in the fall of 1933 the Jacksons moved to Rochester, New York, because of a business venture. The Traung Label and Lithograph Company of San Francisco had merged with the Stecher Company of Rochester; and Mr. Jackson, who had been promoted to represent the Western Division, became its president. The adjustment was a difficult one for Miss Jackson, as there were several disappointments. She entered Brighton High School that fall and hoped, no doubt, to be accepted by certain groups. One short but meaningful diary entry on October 11, 1933, indicates her unhappiness in not achieving what she wished: "I didn't make the sorority — Damn Gene Robbins." But she did not mourn over temporary setbacks, for her determination and resolution for 1934 was "To be Happy." The following June she graduated from Brighton High in the top quarter of her class.

III   *The College Years*

In September, 1934, Shirley Jackson enrolled in the liberal arts program at the University of Rochester. She again suffered periods of depression and unhappiness, perhaps not so much in relation to her studies as in regard to her social life. She made many friends, but there were instances in which she questioned their loyalty. Finally, two years later, in June, 1936, disillusioned with her progress, she withdrew from the university. She had not stopped writing during this period, as her diary attests on February 24, 1935: "Wrote a play tonite which delights me — it is so *myself* — Conceit!" A September note states: "Wrote an allegory which might mean something." She had not lost confidence in her ability to write; in fact, she was more anxious than ever to become a successful author. A November entry of that same year comments: "Story favorable — best I've ever written."

Once free of school, she spent the next year at home as an apprenticeship in writing — which for her meant writing one thousand words a day and establishing work habits she carefully maintained for the remainder of her life; for she was always a conscientious, disciplined writer. By the end of the year, however, she felt the necessity of more schooling and decided to return to college. In the fall of 1937, she entered Syracuse University, where she was at first in the School of Journalism, but transferred later to the department of English. From the first, apparently, her talents and enthusiasm gained attention; sometimes (as will be seen), from the standpoint of the administration and the English department, she won too much attention. All in all, she published fifteen pieces in campus magazines during her two-year stay at Syracuse. Besides her regular English courses, she took abnormal psychology, a meaningful subject in light of its use for her future characterizations of the many tormented people about whom she wrote; in addition, there were her Spanish, sociology, and geology classes. Speech became her minor, but she also took courses in drama and in music. Along with class notes, the pages of her college notebooks contain short poems and penciled cartoon characters.

Professor H. W. Herrington of the English department at

Syracuse, a teacher of Miss Jackson's with whom she had taken "Introduction to Folklore" and "American Folksong," said of her:

> . . . She was the sort of student who was a joy to have in class, alert, active in classroom discussion, communicating the results of her reading to her classmates and to me in papers and conference. . . . She was keenly interested in the topics treated. Some years later, turning the pages of the *New Yorker,* . . . I ran into her remarkable story, "The Lottery," and was so stirred that I immediately wrote her a letter telling her how fine I thought it was. She promptly wrote back saying "But it all originated in your course," which made her old prof very proud that he had directed her to studies which stirred her creative imagination to produce that impressive tale. Among the readings assigned were passages from Brand's *Popular Antiquities* and Frazer's *Golden Bough,* which emphasizes strongly, of course, the traditional rites and customs of the folk, many of them cruel and brutal to the modern taste. . . .[6]

Her first story, "Janice," appeared in the February, 1938, issue of *Threshold,* a magazine sponsored by the creative writing class of the late poet A. E. Johnson. This story supposedly attracted the attention of Stanley Edgar Hyman, a fellow classmate who later became her husband. Later that year, she contributed the first of several stories to the campus humor magazine, *The Syracusan,* to which she was appointed the fiction editor for the year 1939 - 1940. A problem arose when the new editor in chief decided to give the publication a face-lifting by eliminating all short stories. With her position still open, but its function eliminated, she and her colleagues Stanley Edgar Hyman and June Mirken began to plan a magazine of their own, a magazine of literary quality, one that the English Club finally agreed to sponsor. The magazine that emerged was called *The Spectre* from William Blake's lines: "My Spectre before me night and day / like a wild beast guards my way."

The first edition was published in the fall of 1939, and Miss Jackson's humorous editorial relates how the magazine began. As to contributions, she relates that "All the graduates said they wouldn't write for the magazine if it sold a million copies and all the undergraduates said they wouldn't write for the magazine if it were the last magazine on earth. Once we caught a freshman going across campus and we took his English I theme away from him."[7] Actually, they had many contributions; both Miss Jackson and Mr. Hyman, who was now managing editor, were happy to provide stories and essays, and others contributed poetry and artwork. Miss Jackson had, during this year, won second prize in the university poetry contest; and, although her major efforts centered on stories, she had always continued writing poetry.

Their magazine, they determined, would not be slick or professional looking but would represent the best in student writing. As it happened, the first issue, containing fifty mimeographed pages, was ready to be hand bound when a member of the English department who had inspected the pages interrupted proceedings. What occurred next is explained by Miss Jackson in the editorial of the following issue (*Spectre*, Winter, 1940): "Here we are, already a magazine with a lurid past. Just before our first issue was bound, with the pages already mimeographed, the English department (working through our faculty advisor) tapped us on the shoulder gently and informed us that we were a menace to public morals. It seems we had two pictures of nude male bodies, and if you want to have nude bodies in a campus publication, without corrupting morals, they have to be female bodies."

The pictures were removed, but she adds: "What made it particularly funny was that as soon as we went on sale (and as everyone knows, sold out in less time than it would take to burn down the Hall of Languages) the Orange began printing letters from indignant little coeds saying that not only were the rest of our pictures dirty, too, but that our stories weren't anything to show around in mixed company. Which probably shows that even the censors weren't as dirty-minded as they could have been, and which left us with everything offensive but the table of contents."[8]

The magazine continued to be popular, although the administration and the English department may have become increasingly wary of the biting editorials and the various criticisms included in essays. However, a few of the professors contributed material, and among them was Leonard Brown, a teacher of modern literature and criticism as well as a poet and short-story writer. He, apparently, was one of those rare individuals to whom students feel everlastingly grateful; for Miss Jackson devoted almost the entire editorial of the last issue of *The Spectre* (Summer, 1940) to his praises because he had been of immeasurable help in backing the students and the new publication:

He didn't just work for the magazine; he was the magazine. It was his idea and his plans and his opinions we always thought of when we had to make a decision. He taught us that if a 50-page mimeographed magazine could print more student writing than a slick 16-page printed job, it was better, even if it didn't look as pretty. He wrote two or three poems for us that were so good they made us ashamed of some of the standards we had fallen into. When we hit trouble he was the man we came to. If *Spectre* was bad it was our fault and the fault of the student body, but whatever there was good in the magazine came out of Leonard Brown. What we learned from him about writing (and more important, about reading) almost made the years we spent up here worthwhile. He taught us that the aim of reading and criticizing was to know and understand, not to like or dislike, and the aim of writing was to get down what you wanted to say, not to gesticulate or impress.

Her eulogy continues, but she was always to refer to Leonard Brown as her mentor; and in 1959 she dedicated *The Haunting of Hill House* to him. The following year (1960), when he died suddenly, Miss Jackson and Mr. Hyman, with other students, friends, and colleagues, wrote a tribute to him that was incorporated into a memorial essay of praise and appreciation.

Miss Jackson was always sensitive to social ills, and many of these problems became the subjects of her editorials. In this vein, she included one group of angry complaints against the evils of mankind, under the title "Three Sonnets," as follows:

THREE SONNETS
Letter to a Soldier

My dear,

It's lonely now that you are gone, and I grow sick of women and of rain. We all feel strange at being left alone and wonder when the Spring will come again. I have enough to eat, but I have found the seeds you planted will not grow this year — the rain has gone too deep into the ground for anything to grow. Will you be here in time to plant again? The papers said you would be home by summer. When you come bring nothing for the baby. He is dead. The work will be less hard when you are home, but I'm afraid the season will be late for growing things. However, I shall wait.

Man Talks

So what the hell assistance have I been in fixing up this lousy rotten mess? I know damn well this set-up's no success, but who am I among a lot of men? I've got a job, but there are many guys who sit around or bum awhile and wait. Suppose I bitch about the things I hate? Nobody's going to give me any prize.

I got a dollar once when I was broke and begged a man for handouts, and I know the way it feels to be down on your luck. But hell, what can I do? A man once spoke, said guys like me should help the others. So that day I gave a kid a half a buck.

Black Woman's Story

And when they came and took him, I was sure that they'd be hot and weary from the ride and ask him for a drink, and ask me: "You're his new young wife?" and he would smile with pride; Yes, looking at the sky with tightened eyes, and if by chance I spoke they'd turn to me and answer, growing shy like men who talk to women. Yes, I thought they'd come like that, in friendship. But, instead, they came and took and tied him like they'd caught some killing dog, and not a word was said. A neighbor let me know, when it was light, that they had hanged and burned him in the night.

— Shirley Jackson[9]

One discovers in this selection of vignettes an embryo of the same angry young writer who later hoped to shock her readers into the recognition of man's evil in "The Lottery."

As has been said, satire and criticism of mankind are not taken personally and are therefore tolerated; but criticism of an individual or of an institution or of that institution's policies is not well received. Therefore, her editorial in the spring *Spectre* (1940) caused some grumbling. She had entitled the piece "We Stoop to Culture: 22 Propositions Demonstrating the Cultural Level of Syracuse Students." The points began with:

1. They object to the lack of good lighting in the library, but don't bother about the lack of good books.
2. Three times as many students turned out to hear Dorothy Thompson as came to hear Norman Thomas. As long as Phi Beta Kappa wants to honor alumni whose intellectual superiority is in proportion to their newspaper publicity, why not Dixie Davis?

There were also comments about various traditions on campus and several more about the library, such as: "The library thinks that a suitable display of modern American art is a selection of covers, in color, from *Boy's Life* as far back as the year 1926." But perhaps the item that rankled most was a reference to the lack of Negro coeds in the university dormitories: "Marian Anderson sells out every time she comes here, but they won't allow negro coeds in the college dormitories. Maybe it's all right if you're no closer than the sixth row."[10]

The summer, 1940, *Spectre* editorial devotes a fair amount of space to the question of why so few black students were admitted to Syracuse and, again, to the problem of living quarters:

The college is a pretty good place to fight for the rights of the negro people, and this college is a particularly good place. The student branch of the NAACP here has gotten its teeth into the problem of discrimination against negroes in admissions, and the problem of living quarters for them. A cooperative inter-racial house for men will be started next year, and the NAACP right now is investigating the question of negro girls rooming in the cottages and dormitories. All sorts of administrative leaders have been interviewed, and no one seems to know exactly why Syracuse admits so few negroes. The argument that there is no place for them to live falls apart when you look at it. The overwhelming majority of white students on campus have no slightest objection to living with negro students, and would be pretty stupid and bigoted if they did. It would be a waste of space to review all the reasons why college students should learn citizenship and tolerance by living with people of other races, creeds, and colors. It is something that is not a generally accepted educational truth, and the only question is, why doesn't somebody do something about it here? Well, the NAACP is doing something about it, and we wish them all the luck in the world.[11]

All her life Shirley Jackson was to champion the cause of the underdog and to expose prejudice, especially that against Negroes and Jews, as several of her stories attest.

How much ill will these editorials caused within the university administration cannot be assessed; however, the magazine was to receive heavy criticism from another quarter. Stanley Edgar Hyman had been demonstrating his talents by writing critical reviews: "The Misery of Gerard Manley Hopkins: A Criticism," "The Need for a New Poetic Form: An Essay," etc. Such critical articles were acceptable until he reviewed the latest book of poetry by English Professor A. E. Johnson and indicated, unwisely, that several student efforts were superior to his poems. The English department and, understandably, Professor Johnson were furious.

The summer, 1940, issue was the last one of the term; and June Mirken was appointed editor for the coming year since Miss Jackson and Mr. Hyman were graduating. When school began in the fall, however, it was announced that *The Spectre* had been discontinued; and the magazine Miss Jackson and her friends had worked to make a literary and monetary success (it showed a profit) came to an untimely end. Apparently hard feelings on the part of school authorities lasted for quite some time and may have been one of the reasons why neither Miss Jackson, even after becoming a successful author, nor Mr. Hyman, a known critic, was named as a recipient of the Arents Pioneer Medal for outstanding achievement, the highest honor granted by the university. Not until the year of her death in 1965 — twenty-five years later — was the medal finally awarded to her — in absentia, since she was unable to attend the ceremony.

IV   *The Beginning of Two Careers: Marriage and Writing*

The romance between Miss Jackson and Mr. Hyman had progressed steadily during their senior year, and they were married after their graduation on June 3, 1940. Neither of their families was overjoyed about the match, but perhaps the Hymans found it more objectionable. They had hoped that their son might marry a girl of the Jewish faith, and it was some time before they were reconciled to the fact that he had not done so.

After the newlyweds moved to New York City, where he had been appointed an editorial assistant on the staff of *The New Republic*, Miss Jackson continued with her writing and at the same time found herself various clerical jobs. One of these, with Macy's during the Christmas rush, became the source of a short humorous story, "My Life with R. H. Macy," which was published the following December 22, 1941, in *The New Republic*, her first national publication.

In 1942, when Laurence, their first child, was born, Miss Jackson's routine changed drastically; but she continued writing every day. She learned early that the special breed known as the housewife-mother-writer must make important choices and firm decisions. If she looked up from her typewriter and noticed that the windows were dirty, she did not get up and wash them. As a result, *The New Yorker* published the following January (1943) the first of many of her short stories. Called "After You, My Dear Alphonse," it concerns prejudice and erroneous attitudes toward black people. Stanley, in the meantime, had become a staff writer for *The New Yorker*, and, having a husband on the staff of a magazine to which she was contributing material may have been a decided advantage; however, no doubt exists that she was already a skillful and talented professional who sold to the top markets. Her *New Yorker* story "Come Dance With Me in Ireland" was chosen for inclusion in *Best American Short Stories, 1944*. She had sold four stories to *The New Yorker* in 1943; in 1944, they bought four more stories; in addition, *American Mercury* took one; *Mademoiselle*, two; and one story found its way into a collection entitled *Cross-Section*. All in all, she published eight stories during 1944 alone.

V   *Off to Vermont (1945 - 1955)*

Tired of cramped quarters and apartment living in the city, and inspired by friends who had taken to the hills of New Hampshire and Vermont, the Hymans made several trips to search for the ideal location for their growing family. When Mr. Hyman was offered a position at Bennington College, they finally found a suitable house in North Bennington. The search for living quarters, a description of the house, and one of their early years in Vermont later became material for her first book about the family, *Life Among the Savages.* Their daughter Joanne was born this year, 1945, after they had moved to their new home. During the school year, for a time, Miss Jackson was a substitute teacher in creative writing at the college. Although she never tired of talking about writing to interested students in occasional lectures, she did not want to teach and resisted all efforts of the administration in succeeding years to urge her to become a regular faculty member. She was willing to advise students or be a counselor, as indeed she was in later years.

On the surface, 1945 to 1947 were less productive years since she published fewer stories during this period; actually, she had begun a more ambitious project: she was now occupied with her first novel, *The Road Through the Wall*, the California story that was published by Farrar, Straus in 1948. Nineteen forty-eight was to be an important year in her life, for some of her most noteworthy stories were written during it. "The Lottery" appeared (with much fanfare later) in the June 26, 1948, issue of *The New Yorker;* and, as has been said many times, if Shirley Jackson had written nothing else, she would still be famous for this one work. "Charles," another much-anthologized story, appeared in the July issue of *Mademoiselle;* "Pillar of Salt," in the October issue of the same magazine; "Renegade," in the November issue of *Harper's Magazine;* "The Tooth," in the *Hudson Review;* and "Seven Types of Ambiguity," in the fall issue of *Story Magazine.* Mr. Hyman had not been teaching since 1946, for he, too, had been working on a significant project although he was still writing for *The New Yorker.* His study of modern literary critics, *The Armed Vision*, also appeared in 1948 and was hailed by men of letters as an important contribution in the field of literary criticism.

During this same year, the Hymans added another daughter to their family when Sarah (Sally) was born. Somehow, despite duties she could not ignore — some housework, the care of the children, the cooking of meals, and the chauffeuring chores — Miss Jackson kept regular writing hours. When the children were small, the stolen hours were in the evening; when they were older, she chose the morning while they were at school. At times, when a story idea came suddenly, she would hurry off to her typewriter. A friend, Mrs. Thomas H. Foster, remembers one evening in particular when a group was playing Monopoly at the Hymans. Miss Jackson, apparently, was as good at Monopoly as she was at most games; however, she suddenly began to sell her property and then left for her study. The game was still going on when she reappeared with a story; she read it aloud to the group, listened to the various comments, and then returned to her study to retype the portions she had decided to change. By the time the game was over and the guests were ready to leave, the story was in an envelope, ready to go to her agent.

The publication of "The Lottery" brought fame, as well as letters from readers from all over the country and from many parts of the world. There were notes of praise, as she has stated, but more often abusive letters from people who did not understand her motives or what she was trying to do. The following year, Farrar, Straus and Company published a collection of her short stories; featuring "The Lottery," this book was entitled *The Lottery, or The Adventures of James Harris*. The critics had, by this time, decided that Shirley Jackson was a writer of much talent; they recognized her uniqueness. After an interview in 1949 with Miss Jackson for the *New York Times Book Review*, writer Harvey Breit made the following comments:

Magic is the word that has been woven around the literary personality of Shirley Jackson, the latest to join the select corps of triumphant women short-story writers who apparently flourish in America. Of the stories that make up her surprisingly high-selling collection — entitled "The Lottery" — critics have said they signaled a return to an era of witchcraft and magic; the supernatural and some sort of devil worship. One critic went so far as to say that Miss Jackson wrote not with a pen but with a broomstick. . . .
This, as the phrase commonly goes, may or may not be. To the uncosmological eye, Miss Jackson . . . looks not only wholesome but very much on the dayside. She is neat, detached and impersonally warm. She subtly radiates an atmosphere of coziness and comfort, and appears to be of a tranquil disposition. All in all, Miss Jackson looks like a mother. . . . She does indeed use a broomstick, but for household chores rather than as a means of transportation.

True, Miss Jackson believes in magic. She says it works for her, both the black and white varieties. But she also says it's a silly thing to talk about. Obviously, Miss Jackson was able to be natural even about the supernatural.

As for her views about writing, Mr. Breit says:

Writing in general, she says, short stories in particular are perhaps nearest and dearest to her heart. But it is as a mother — and not as a witch — that she approaches the heart of the matter. "I can't persuade myself," Miss Jackson said, "that writing is honest work. It is a very personal reaction, but 50 per cent of my life is spent washing and dressing the children, cooking, washing dishes and clothes and mending. After I get it all to bed, I turn around to my typewriter and try to — well, to create concrete things again. It's great fun, and I love it. But it doesn't tie any shoes."

As Shirley explained to Mr. Breit, she did not fight writing as Stanley did and as many writers do; she found it relaxing. In regard to her literary likes, she confessed that she did not appreciate the nineteenth century, for that age is "moody and touchy and it broods too much." She preferred the eighteenth century: "I like eighteenth-century novels, Richardson and Fanny Burney. Everyone should be made to read 'Pamela.' Richardson — nobody believes me — but there's a tremendous sense of leisure and peace in him, and he wrote just for the love of it. He just took a really rich, deep pleasure in doing it."[12] In the interview, she also indicated that she considered Katherine Anne Porter and Elizabeth Bowen to be the best modern writers in her own genre.

In 1949, Miss Jackson sold several family stories to the women's magazines, especially *Good Housekeeping* and *Woman's Home Companion*. Her gift for casual, humorous storytelling gained many readers and demonstrated that she could write in many styles and in many moods. Whether this range of talent was, in the long run, a handicap is difficult to say; for money was an issue — and the funny family tales sold well. There are, after all, few good writers of humor, and humor is always in demand; but, unfortunately, most funny stories are soon forgotten or are not regarded seriously. The Hymans had developed a habit of reading and discussing each other's work. Mr. Hyman had once said that, while he could not write a short story, he could, once given the material, shape and refine it. An excellent critic, he was impressed with most of his wife's work, but he considered the family chronicles "potboilers."

In 1949, the Hymans moved to Westport, Connecticut, ostensibly to be closer to New York; but comments have indicated that they were disturbed by a certain amount of anti-Semitism in North Bennington. There was no doubt that many Vermont natives considered the college people to be a rather strange breed of human, although little distinction seems to have been made between Jewish and Gentile faculty members; but the villagers who knew and dealt with Miss Jackson liked her immensely. Since she ran the errands, did the shopping, and picked up the daily papers (they took several) at the small store that also served as a taxi station, she got to know several of the local people quite well. They appreciated her friendliness and her sense of humor; indeed, everyone who knew her said that she was a very funny person, very witty, very bright.

The Hymans did not appreciate Westport as much as they had hoped; but she was, as usual, working hard: during 1950, she published six stories in various magazines including *The New Mexico Quarterly Review, Collier's,* and *The Reader's Digest* (which did a reprint of the "Charles" story). In 1951, her second novel *Hangsaman* was ready for publication, and critics regarded it favorably, it being hailed by some, including the *Time* magazine staffer and the writer of *The Yale Review,* as one of the outstanding books of the year.[13] Two years in Westport were enough to convince the Hymans of the beauties of Vermont, one of which, no doubt, was that Bennington was farther from New York; for by this time Miss Jackson disliked the city intensely, visiting it only when necessary. Back in North Bennington, they made two temporary moves before locating in the fourteen-room house on upper Main Street which they eventually called home.

At this time, Miss Jackson was invited to lecture for the first time at the Breadloaf Writers' Conference, but she was already an experienced lecturer, having been involved regularly since 1949 with the Marlboro and Cummington Fiction Conferences. She also received an offer to teach writing at Smith College — in fact, to take Mary Ellen Chase's position since Miss Chase was to retire. Only mildly interested, Miss Jackson journeyed to Northampton for the interview with Miss Chase, who was to select her own successor. Shirley Jackson enjoyed the interview, but she felt a bit stifled and uneasy in the atmosphere; in fact, it may have been that she was tired from the drive, or that she was pregnant, or that she had fortified herself with a cocktail at lunch, or all three — at any rate, she fainted; and, when she had sufficiently recovered, she thanked Miss Chase and graciously declined the position.

For the Hyman family, the most important event of the year was the birth of their fourth child and second son, Barry. His antics were soon to become an essential part of the second family chronicle, *Raising Demons*. Having four children did nothing to hamper Miss Jackson's literary activities, but she was a careful and considerate mother and, apparently, a wonderful cook. As their former neighbors, Mr. and Mrs. Murry Karmiller, said about her:

She was more than dedicated, rose at 5:30 or 6:30 A.M. to fix breakfast for the family, taxied them to school until they were old enough to walk to school alone, saw them as part of the community, baked mountains of brownies for them, for volunteer fire department bake sales (often enough, we would come into our own kitchen around 8 in the morning to find Shirley waiting for us with a fresh batch of cookies or brownies — almost to the day she died), and encouraged the children to join Little League, the Scouts, etc.[14]

She must have had tremendous resources of energy, for it was during these years, the 1950's, when her children were growing up that her literary output was the greatest: at least forty-four short stories were published during this decade (many of these, however, are the family-based stories for the women's magazines); six articles; two book-length family chronicles; one children's nonfiction book; and four novels.

In 1952, eleven of her stories appeared in magazines: three in *Harper's*; others in *Good Housekeeping, Woman's Home Companion, Collier's, Woman's Day*; and one in a *New World Writing* anthology. This year also "The Lottery" was adapted by Ellen Violett for television, and appeared in the anthology of *Best Television Plays*. In 1953, Miss Jackson was represented by ten stories and by the publication of the first family book, *Life Among the Savages,* which *The Reader's Digest* also featured in its condensed books. This year, too, "The Lottery" was adapted by Brainerd Duffield into play form; it became for the next several years one of the most performed one-act plays by little theater and high-school groups.

The routine of family life changed again significantly when Mr. Hyman once again became in 1953 a professor at Bennington College. Since he did not drive, Miss Jackson arranged her schedule in order to take him to and from his office. Mr. Hyman was, it seems, a stimulating teacher, and his course "Myth and Ritual in Literature" soon became, and remained, until his death, the most popular course at Bennington. He, too, was a disciplined writer who was methodical in his work schedule; for instance, on Mondays he wrote his "Talk of the Town" *New Yorker* material; on Tuesdays, he attended to correspondence, etc.

As a faculty wife, Miss Jackson tried to avoid involvement in college activities as long as it was possible; but she later participated in various committees and also published a funny account of what it meant to be a faculty wife in *Mademoiselle* (December, 1956). The article had been written for the college alumnae magazine and was to be on display during graduation week, but, because the account included reference to student drinking, certain of the "alums" preferred to keep the magazine out of sight — an action that infuriated Miss Jackson, who could not abide hypocrisy in any form. Her indignation caused her to send the story to her agent, who immediately sold it to *Mademoiselle*.

For the Hymans, the big literary event of 1954 was the publication of her novel *The Bird's Nest*, which received very good reviews. Both *Hangsaman* and *The Bird's Nest* are indications of her keen interest in the workings of the mind, and it may have been during this period that she herself first suffered moments of anxiety that became more intense as the years progressed. After Metro-Goldwyn-Mayer indicated an interest in making a movie of *The Bird's Nest*, negotiations extended through the following year until the contract was drawn up; and not long thereafter Metro-Goldwyn-Mayer produced the film under the title *Lizzie*. Its release came shortly before that of a movie similar in theme — also on multiple personalities but based on a different case study — *The Three Faces of Eve*.

About this time the University of California wrote to Miss Jackson, requesting that she, as an alumna, consider giving her manuscripts to it, a proposal that startled her somewhat since she had never been a student there. She finally deduced that they had mistaken her for Helen Hunt Jackson. Later, when Syracuse University made a similar request, she again declined, perhaps still harboring resentment about the death of *The Spectre* and the lack of recognition given her by the university. As it turned out, the problem of the manuscripts was not resolved until Mr. Hyman donated them to the Library of Congress in 1968, three years after his wife's death.

VI   *Interest in the Occult*

During 1955 Miss Jackson published few stories. One of these, however, "One Ordinary Day With Peanuts," was later chosen for *Best American Short Stories, 1956*. In the meantime, she had been asked to write a nonfiction book for young people about the Salem witchcraft trials. Her publicity after "The Lottery" indicated that she had witchlike propensities, and she jokingly proclaimed herself the only practicing witch in New England. Her private collection of demonology, she admitted, consisted of some five hundred books from many countries. Some of the works were in languages she could not even read, but there was no doubt of her long-time fascination with the topic of superstition. As has been observed, her childhood diary had shown her inclination to view events in terms of luck and of good and evil omens. Apparently, her active search for knowledge of the occult began in the Rochester years; and, by the time Miss Jackson had transferred to Syracuse, according to her friend June Mirken (now Mrs. June Mintz), Miss Jackson was already familiar with a good bit of literature in the field of demonology and was particularly interested in the history of the black mass. "She also owned a Tarot pack and a ouija board, with which she experimented."[15]

Later, at Bennington, her friends said that she told fortunes at the college fairs and that she was especially good with the Tarot cards; but sometimes she was selective about whom she would read for. She was, apparently, very sensitive and intuitive, besides being highly imaginative and superstitious. The Hymans' good friend, poet Howard Nemerov, recalls one instance where "she told me to leave the house for criticizing one of Stanley's essays — at his request. She said I was hexing his chances of selling it to *The New Yorker*. Stanley intervened to protect me by saying he could fight his own battles. But the seriousness, and indeed a touch of malevolence, was real enough."[16] For her, there would always be mysteries one could not expose to daylight or explain in ordinary terms.

Probably one of Miss Jackson's more pleasant tasks was the writing of *The Witchcraft of Salem Village* (1956), a nonfiction Landmark book designed for the twelve-to-fourteen-year-old reader. When Bennet Cerf expressed interest in publishing a book about Salem witchcraft, Miss Jackson's agent contacted her. The result was a very readable and knowledgeable book. The first chapter presents a simplified history of witchcraft that includes several interesting items such as the fact that in mid-sixteenth century a French scholar had said that he had discovered the exact number of the devil's army. There were 7,409,127 demons, he said, that were commanded by seventy-nine demonic princes who were responsible to the devil himself; but a later scholar claimed to have discovered a still larger number of demonic spirits.

Miss Jackson's discussion leads to the Satan-fearing atmosphere of Salem, Massachusetts, and Salem Village, two separate places only a few miles apart. The Puritans, she explains, felt that Satan was especially desirous of destroying *them*; and, since the devil could take many forms and enlist the aid of many people, the Puritans felt constantly surrounded by witches and evil spirits. This fear of witches in both England and America resulted in the executions of two million people by the end of the eighteenth century.

VII   *Other Activities of the Later Years (1956 - 1965)*

Besides *The Witchcraft of Salem Village*, Miss Jackson had also published five short stories in 1956. Most of these were family stories, and then in 1957 her second family chronicle, *Raising Demons*, appeared. Many of the previously published domestic accounts were included in this book and in its predecessor, *Life Among the Savages*. Her own work schedule continued to be staggering, for in a letter to her mother of June 16, 1958, she states that, during the past three weeks, she had written one children's play, three stories, and one-third of a novel. She had also been chosen this year to be Chairman of the Faculty Wives Committee and had been asked again to join the faculty of Bennington College. Her answer to the college was the usual rejection, for the idea of a regular teaching job terrified her. The children's play *The Bad Children*, originally written for Joanne and Sally with songs for which Laurie wrote the music, was published by the Dramatic Publishing Company in 1958. This one-act play was a spoof on both witchcraft and the Hansel and Gretel story. She enjoyed working with plays, intended to write more, but never had time to do so. The novel turned out to be *The Sundial*, which was published in the latter part of the year.

And there were, as always, certain community activities besides the Little League games that Miss Jackson and her friend Peg Wohnus attended since their sons were active players. She was cooperative in fund-raising activities for the Parent-Teachers Association. On one occasion, however, she helped with a musical called *All Aboard* until she discovered that the last act was to be performed in blackface. Then she was furious, and, protesting loudly, would have nothing more to do with the show. When her daughters were a bit older, so that they, too, might benefit, she volunteered to conduct a short-story writing course at the high school in the late afternoons.

She was still lecturing during the summers at writers' conferences. The previous summer (1957) she had returned to Syracuse University for the first time to participate in a writing workshop and had been happy, apparently, to see Professor Leonard Brown again. At times, the Hymans combined their speaking engagements, lecturing at the same schools but on different topics. His subject was, most often, anthropology. During the summer when there were no speaking engagements, Miss Jackson enjoyed attending the races at Saratoga; otherwise, she remained at home where she was happiest and felt the safest.

She wrote several articles for *Good Housekeeping* during 1959, besides a short story for *The Saturday Evening Post*, and an article on children's books for *The Reporter*; but the significant literary event was the publication of her notable "ghost story" (as she called it), *The Haunting of Hill House*, dedicated to Leonard Brown. This book was the first to be published by the Viking Press; for she and Farrar, Straus had dissolved their contract. *Hill House*, having received excellent reviews, went through several printings and was purchased by *The Reader's Digest* for its condensed books. Four years later, under the title *The Haunting*, it became a successful movie, starring Julie Harris and Claire Bloom.

In one of Miss Jackson's letters to her mother (undated, but written around this time), she states that the Hymans had been giving dinner parties once a week. They had always been excellent hosts, gracious, "wildly generous," and fun-loving. Through the years their guests had included many notable novelists, poets, critics, musicians, educators, and other professional men and women. Bennington has always attracted a brilliant faculty, and most of those seem to have appreciated the Hymans. Among the distinguished faculty and good friends of the Hymans were Bernard Malamud, Ralph Ellison, Howard Nemerov, Kenneth Burke, and Ben Belitt. Many of the group seem to have been avid bridge players; and, for a period of fifteen years, every Thursday night a men's poker game took place. Mr. Hyman was a member with many of the faculty, two local doctors, a garageman, and the (then) president of the college. The location of the party rotated from home to home; but everyone remembers Mrs. Hyman's hospitality, her good food, and her attention (when required), even if she were busy at the typewriter. Years later when the parties were over, after Mr. Hyman had died suddenly of a heart attack (1970), poet Howard Nemerov wrote "Myth & Ritual," a eulogy that uses the metaphor of the poker game.

Through the years, Miss Jackson had gained a great deal of weight. She had asthma and, later, arthritis in the ends of her fingers. Worse yet, she had begun to suffer from attacks of anxiety. Always a nervous and rather tense person, she was now under the care of a psychiatrist. For a time, she found even shopping impossible and tended to remain in seclusion more and more. But, even during the worst periods, she never stopped working; she used her typewriter as therapy — to write pages and pages of anything she pleased to unburden herself of the depressions into which she sank. At this point, for her, all social activities ceased. The early 1960's were difficult years. Nevertheless, she wrote three articles during 1960, one for *Playboy*; and she collaborated on a book for mothers-to-be, *Special Delivery,* which was a collection of short essays, most of them humorous — a publishing venture with which she was not pleased. The introduction describes this work as: "a useful book for brand new mothers in which Shirley Jackson as chief resident provides a sane and sage approach to the hilarious and homey situations which accompany the advent of motherhood — aided by a well-tried staff of specialists including Mark Twain, Cornelia Otis Skinner, Robert Benchley, B. J. Chute, Ogden Nash, and other interested parties."[17]

Miss Jackson contributed to the volume thirteen short articles that supply common sense along with the fun. In such chapters as "Doing What Comes Naturally," the Hymans' cat Ninki with her newborn kittens serves as a springboard for suggestions that mothers should not be afraid to trust to their own logic in bringing up children; and in "How to Make a Husband a Father," she reminds the reader that it takes two to cope with baby. If necessary, mother can indulge in a third martini if baby's crying becomes too irritating. Everything need not go like clockwork. Also, although one cannot count on fathers to take over feeding, a husband can be reassuring, comforting, and patient. Another article, "Who is Boss?," is a brief note on discipline versus permissiveness with Miss Jackson on the side of some disciplining. While these pieces are light and, undoubtedly, mildly helpful to young mothers, Miss Jackson was right in judging them as no asset to her literary career. The humorist discovers that his playful whims are often fine for the moment but too slight for permanent wear.

Two articles appeared in *Good Housekeeping* in 1961. These housewifely pieces, casual and delightfully whimsical, are similar in tone to the family chronicles. For instance, "What I Want to Know Is, What Do Other People Cook With?" is an account of her search for a little black-handled, four-tined kitchen fork like the one her mother gave her many years before. No one else has cooked with one, apparently, nor can she find one in a store anywhere. As she says, "I took to hanging around people's kitchens, a habit which made me fairly unpopular and eventually got us largely not invited out to dinner any more, trying to find out how other people do things." Then, she says, she paid $5.95 for a "great unwieldy thing that flipped porkchops halfway across the kitchen and short-circuited the toaster and could have been used nicely for weeding the garden."[18] Finally, in a basement store in Brooklyn, a friend finds such a fork for the huge sum of one dollar — because it was a rarity, she says; the original had cost her mother twenty-five cents.

Another of her popular articles is one written for *The Saturday Evening Post* (June 6, 1964) "No, I Don't Want to Go to Europe." The opinions behind this piece were not entirely truthful, for the Hymans had been planning a trip to Europe that had then been postponed until some future date. The article, therefore, is a rather tongue-in-cheek one, an intellectual exercise in the reasons why one should stay home. Miss Jackson would not fly and did not like boats. When she traveled at all, she preferred a car. As for Europe, she states that she was sure that she would not like the food, the traffic, the passports, the buses, the walking, the souvenirs, the other tourists, the money problems, the clothes, or the wine. In fact, she says, she was mortally afraid of practically everything, which at this stage in her life may have been a fairly accurate assessment. This article, like her others, is original and provides entertaining reading.

During these years she was at work on another novel, which she had begun in 1959. The writing went slowly; but three years later, when *We have Always Lived in the Castle* was finished, it made the best-seller list, and *Time* magazine named it one of the ten best novels of the year. After much persuasion, Miss Jackson agreed to travel to New York for the publication festivities, which included interviews, luncheon at Sardi's, and a cocktail party at the St. Regis. Whether serious or not, she confided to her mother that she was not anxious for a book award or a Pulitzer Prize, nor did she want the ex-

tra money. Her husband, chief bookkeeper of the family, had stated
that a movie sale on this book would "finish them." Apparently,
there had been many tax complications resulting from the domestic
and foreign sales of books and stories, and these problems had been
intensified by the sale of the movie rights to *The Bird's Nest* and *The
Haunting of Hill House*. As it happened, plans were made for a
Broadway production of *We Have Always Lived in the Castle*. Four
years later in 1966, the year after Miss Jackson's death, the un-
successful play version opened on Broadway and lasted only four
days.

Even when Miss Jackson was ill, the Hyman household was one of
good conversation on a wide range of topics from English kings to
anthropological studies; and books were a necessary part of their
lives. Both Miss Jackson and Mr. Hyman were intensely interested in
many subjects, and for a time they took turns at reading the Bible
aloud every evening after dinner. For diversion, besides the
eighteenth-century novels and the works on demonology, Miss
Jackson loved mystery stories; and she bought all the pocket editions
that the local stores offered, even though Mr. Hyman did not ap-
prove. Their home literally bulged with books, for by this time their
library contained more than thirty thousand volumes. Along with
the books, there was Mr. Hyman's growing coin collection which, by
the 1960's, had an estimated value of almost $100,000.

As were her writing and her reading, music was a type of therapy
for Miss Jackson; and at this time she and her neighbor, Barbara
Karmiller, were playing piano duets, just as she and Dorothy Ayling
had once done in the Burlingame days. Mr. Karmiller recalls the environment of the Hyman home: "Along with the four children and
steady stream of guests there were at times five cats and two dogs.
There were birds, fish, and, until he ran himself out, a hamster. The
hamster's cage sat on the piano; it delighted Shirley to see him
change his running speed to suit the tempo of the music being
played. Often Shirley and Barbara played duets; the programs
usually were diversified and went from Bach to corny snow-flake-
and-sled songs. She treasured a song book that had the Groucho
Marx Captain Spaulding number in it, and we all enjoyed singing
with her."[19]

In 1963, Miss Jackson finished a children's picture book, *Nine
Magic Wishes*, one of a series of "Modern Masters Books for
Children." Other authors contributing to the series were Arthur
Miller, Robert Graves, John Ciardi, Phyllis McGinley, Conrad

Aiken, and William Saroyan. Miss Jackson's keen sense of humor and her lively imagination were valuable assets in this field and would have ensured her success if she had chosen to concentrate on children's literature. She was, at the same time, reviewing children's books for the *New York Herald Tribune.* This year, it seems, was the worst in her illness, but she began to improve gradually. She still made appearances at conferences, and she was a member of the teaching staff at the Breadloaf Writers' Conference from August 12 to 26, 1964. She was also a guest lecturer at Columbia and then later at a New York State teachers' convention. Strangely, while she did not feel confident enough to go shopping alone or to be in large groups of people, her particular neurosis was not disturbed by these activities. Nineteen sixty-four was her least productive year, with the publication of only one article, in *The Saturday Evening Post*; Mr. Hyman, on the other hand, finished another critical book, *The Promised End*, for which he received considerable praise.

In April, 1965, Miss Jackson and Mr. Hyman returned to Syracuse University as guest lecturers for the eighth annual Festival of Arts. A headline in the April 26 issue of the *Daily Orange* states: "Writer in Exile: Shirley Jackson Returns." Both she and Mr. Hyman gave formal lectures and then spoke to individual English classes. She read from several of her works: "The Lottery," an excerpt from *Come Along With Me* (a novel in progress), and a section from an unfinished children's book. The *Daily Orange* gives the following description of the occasion: "Dressed in a bright red dress, with her long hair streaming down her back, Miss Jackson read slowly and carefully; at times, especially during her reading of 'Come Along With Me,' she was interrupted by loud laughter from the audience."[20] They appreciated her wit. As a result of an interview with her, a student correspondent says of her writing habits: "Today she tries to keep a schedule of writing from 9 to 12 every morning, although Miss Jackson claims she tries 'any possible excuse for not getting those ten pages done.' She expects to complete the two books currently in progress by next spring."[21]

Come Along With Me, the comic novel on which Shirley Jackson was working when she died, was to be quite different, apparently, from any of her other novels. Although it includes supernatural elements, they are treated humorously. The completed sections appear, along with several hitherto uncollected short stories, in the anthology *Come Along With Me*, edited by Mr. Hyman. For the first time — aside from the family chronicles — the protagonist is quite like the author herself, a mature woman (age forty-four, size forty-four) with a great deal of imagination and a sense of humor; and she is free for the first time in her life to live where and how she pleases. In the story her artist husband has recently died — to her relief; and she has a bit of money with which to go to a small, strange city to meet people and to start life over again; she is starved for strangers, she says.

Miss Jackson once commented that it was difficult to make people understand that, after twenty years of being with family, she now enjoyed going places alone, stopping to talk to people, or looking at houses. In the same way, the heroine of *Come Along With Me* is sampling life for the first time, an experience she finds exhilarating. Establishing the rules for her life as she has need for them, she is often governed by fancies and whims that suit her extraordinary nature. For example, she decides at one point to try her hand at shoplifting but then realizes that she has no talents in this direction; her real profession, she tells people, is dabbling with the supernatural. She has discovered psychic tendencies within herself since the initial appearance of spirit voices ("Find Rosalind Bleeker. Tell her Sid says hello") when she was twelve years old; thereafter, she often sees people and objects that others cannot see. This ability gives her certain advantages but sets her apart as being strange. Although Mrs. Motorman (the protagonist) is a delightful character, one cannot sense Miss Jackson's plans for her; the existing sections serve as an introduction and little else.

Daily living was now becoming more bearable for Miss Jackson; her anxieties were disappearing; she was well on the way to recovery. Her sessions with the psychiatrist were tapering off. The sad fact was that, though the mind was well again, the body was not. Mr. Hyman, however, had had a heart attack; and he seemed to have the poorer health of the two. On the afternoon of August 8, 1965, a lazy Sunday afternoon, Miss Jackson went upstairs to take her usual nap; she instructed Sally to wake her at four o'clock; and, when four o'clock came, Sally tried to wake her but could not. Miss Jackson had died peacefully in her sleep.

She had always feared death, just as she feared pain; and both she and Mr. Hyman had unorthodox wishes about their exits from the world. Their unwritten pact was that they be cremated and that there be no funeral and no flowers. As the *Bennington Banner* of August 9 states: "In accordance with her wishes, there will be no funeral service. In lieu of flowers, the family has suggested that friends who desire may make contributions in her memory to Bennington College Library Fund."[22] When Howard Nemerov wrote a short memorial for her, he gave a general appraisal of her works: "Miss Jackson was a fabulist. That is, in an age whose most praised novels are given to descriptions of how it feels to sit on a real toilet seat, she told her fables of the real and abstract life, which takes place equally in the fact and in the mind which alone is able to read the fact."[23] At the conclusion he states: " 'My friends,' Chekhov said, looking in at a party, 'you live badly.' Shirley Jackson, too, with that somewhat frighteningly purified vision that can see how badly we live has told us with great brilliance and strength that we live badly; but she has always said to us also, 'My friends'!"[24]

VIII   *Memories*

Of her childhood and the memories of her mother Shirley Jackson, Joanne (Jai) Schnurer writes:

. . . although she wasn't what anyone could rationally call beautiful she was an extraordinarily charming woman and throughout my childhood there were hundreds of people who partied at our house and came to see her for the pleasure of rapping with her. Everyone would always follow her into the kitchen and settle down while she made dinner or whatever. They (later including us) would drink and gossip and tell stories to discredit themselves and each other and always everybody would laugh a great deal. My mother loved to sing and when we cleaned up the kitchen she and my sister and I (sometimes our brothers) would sing as loudly and as famously as we could and often the people who were "guests" would settle around the kitchen table again and sing too . . .
. . . Shirley would tell us stories of the royal houses of England, entrancing us by making the histories as real as our own lives. Sometimes in exchange we could get her outside to jump rope, which she was surprisingly good at. She used to like to stand out on the porch on summer nights when a storm was coming up, it was cooler, and I think she liked the drama of the thunder and lightning; we would yell as loud as we could back at the storm. When it finally did rain we would sometimes run off the porch and dash around getting soaked; Shirley would stand on the porch until it got cooler and then go in and sit in the study with my father and read.

Of the difficult times, referring to her mother's illness, she says:

I remember the process of her getting her nerve back in public; she would say "I think I can go into the Grand Union today, they have some smoked cheese which your father most particularly would like" and we would park in the lot and go in, directly to the cheese. (We weren't messing around; we both knew it was really hard for her and we both knew it was absurdly easy for me.) Sometimes she would get in and have to leave fast and I would finish the errand. Later sometimes she would say she thought she could go in alone or that, she thought it was all right to park here and *walk across the street* to get something and we both would be real glad she could make whatever particular test it was she had set. You understand I was maybe 14 and I accepted a lot of this without seeing it as especially remarkable, nobody else's mother was the least bit like her anyway, so I didn't really feel too weird about doing the outside things with her. We got to be pretty close, maybe I escaped some of the mother-daughter thing with her because of these trips, she never ended up patronizing me or putting me down because I was an adolescent; we were sort of equals, maybe. We certainly did talk more satisfyingly than my friends and I ever did.[25]

A friend of Shirley's relates:

The one thing Shirley did do for herself, because it related to her work, was take a nap every day. Early on it was made clear to everyone that no one was to phone the house between one and three p.m. She really did sleep then, so she could drink and stay up till all hours and fix all those meals for all the family plus those parties. Food at Hyman parties was worth dreaming about. In the later fifties, the parties became less frequent, and less fun. I guess we were all getting older, wiser, sadder. Too much time had been spent playing poker that should have been spent working.

In regard to Shirley and Stanley, she adds: "Shirley had the highest respect for Stanley as a writer, as her critic, and as the head of the household. His word always was law. In his way he was extremely disciplined and dictatorial."[26] Regarding her father, Mrs. Schnurer recalls:

. . . it was Shirley who turned me on to mysteries, we both loved them and read all we could and both got a lot of grief from Stanley about it. I liked him very much, he was terribly smart and I think he knew everything. I always thought he tried very hard to be honest and fair with his kids, the only trouble was that we were not at all interested in getting a lot of education and doing great and wise things, which disappointed him very much, but he knew he had to let us do what we wanted in the end. Finally he would give up and sigh and eventually he would talk about something else about which we didn't disagree. He was a pretty jolly man; he liked especially to laugh, we all did; we used to have joke-telling contests at dinner. Sometimes Stanley would tell us stories and parables like Greek and Roman myths; I remember the story about the man walking towards the wall whose steps are each half of the preceding step; I remember it took a long time for Stanley to convince us that he never really can reach the wall.[27]

Apparently the Hymans' marriage had been a happy one, although there were difficult periods, especially in the early years. As a friend says of them, they were quite dependent on each other; they needed each other's advice, criticism, moral support, and love.

CHAPTER 2

The Short Stories

M ISS Jackson, who first acquired fame through her short
stories, quickly became known as a talented and prolific
writer. At the end of her career, even after several successful novels,
she was still best known as the author of the short stories and of "The
Lottery" in particular. Before dealing with the characteristics of her
style — her straightforward manner of presentation, her use of symbolism; her irony; and her treatment of ambiguity, mystery, and
suspense — one should examine the variety of themes that are the
subject of her tales.

I   *Themes*

One easily thinks of Miss Jackson's creations as "tales" since, even
in the serious works, one suspects that her primary purpose is to
entertain. The fact that she is, as will be seen, a master storyteller
does not deny the truth and validity of her message. Her insights and
observations about man and society are disturbing; and in the case of
"The Lottery," they are shocking. The themes themselves are not
new: evil cloaked in seeming good; prejudice and hypocrisy;
loneliness and frustration; psychological studies of minds that have
slipped the bonds of reality; studies of persons subjected to suspense
and terror; and the humorous helplessness of parents in the in-
evitable crises of family living. As indicated, these themes may not
be new, but her treatment of them often is. She creates microcosms,
private worlds set apart from the larger universe of crowds and cities,
pushing-and-shoving functional people; away from the problems of
ecology and population growth and urban housing renewal. Even in
the tales of family life, the experiences are almost entirely confined
within the limits of the house, and they center on the mother who is,
of course, Shirley Jackson herself. Neither is "The Lottery," a story
of community social evil, exempt from presentation as an isolated

world; for, as typical of other communities as this particular village is meant to be, it is pictured as almost isolated from the rest of mankind, which is also basically unenlightened, narrow, and evil.

The isolation, the loneliness, and the frustrations that plague Miss Jackson's characters have many causes; but one of the major sources, and one of her favorite topics, is mental illness — a subject that she knew well, for she had suffered from bouts of depression and anxiety for years. However, she had always been fascinated with the shadowy world of the mind, with the powers the mind controls, and with the confusion that results from disturbed thoughts and repressed anxieties. She sees the psychotic and emotionally disturbed as victims of some demonic spirit whose capricious nature feeds on loneliness and unhappiness. And, though man manufactures many of his own problems, evils exist over which he has little control; among these are his own fears. His anxieties trap him. As a result, her people — those whose vision of reality is no longer clear-cut — are very much alone.

In the psychological stories (the critics term them "thrillers"), Miss Jackson's protagonists suffer varying degrees of anxiety. In the more advanced stages, they are unaware of what is happening to them until one day nothing in the real world is significant or meaningful; and they find themselves powerless in a tangle of dreams and shadows. Occasionally, the reader is allowed to share the author's secret, to witness the disintegration of a troubled mind; more often the reader is startled into the discovery that all is not well, and the heroine's flight into fantasy comes as something of a surprise, but Miss Jackson's workmanship is such that a review of past events reveals that the signs have been there all along. Suspense is created by the unpredictability of the character's behavior.

In the story "The Beautiful Stranger" (1946), the reader is warned at the outset to expect the unusual: "What might be called the first intimation of strangeness occurred at the railroad station. She had come with her children, Smalljohn and her baby girl, to meet her husband when he returned from a business trip to Boston."[1] Through the anxious eyes of Margaret, a young housewife, the reader explores the unusual situation in which she finds herself. One learns that not only has the young couple quarreled before John left for Boston, but also that theirs has been a home of tension and — on Margaret's part, at least — ill will. While John's thoughts are never revealed, Margaret's show her to be tense and afraid. At the station, her odd sensations increase; and the homecoming is marred also by

Smalljohn's unruly behavior and by the baby's screaming rejection of her father.

Later, at home, Margaret is suddenly struck with the idea that this man is not her husband but a beautiful stranger who, for some unknown but perfectly logical reason, has come to take John's place. Since the thought is exciting to her, she willingly entertains the man, convinced that he is aware of her discovery and is — at the same time — enjoying the deception as much as she is. She tests him with a few questions; and, while the reader sees that the answers are inconclusive, Margaret is happily convinced that the man is not John. He doesn't look quite like John, she decides; his hair is a little darker; his hands, a bit stronger. Suspense increases, for the reader knows that something is amiss; but, at this point, he cannot assess the situation or judge the direction of future events, as the laws of logic and probability seem to be inoperative.

Margaret's obsession persists, and she is happy for the first time in many months. The following day (home from the office), John remarks, "Someone told me today . . . that he had heard I was back from Boston, and I distinctly thought he said that he heard I was dead in Boston." She replies, "At any rate, . . . *you* were not dead in Boston, and nothing else matters" (p. 71). But the reader is perplexed. Is this an element of fantasy; has a dead husband returned? The uncertainty the reader experiences at this point is characteristic of the reaction to events in many of the stories.

Shirley Jackson keeps her audience guessing. Increasingly pleased with her stranger, Margaret is sad when it is time for him to leave for the office. On the afternoon of the second day, instead of taking the children to the park as usual, she calls a baby-sitter, takes a taxi into town to shop for a gift for him, and enjoys wandering about the strange shops "choosing small lovely things." Since it is almost dark when she returns, she indicates to the driver what she believes to be her home; but, when the taxi leaves and she walks toward the house, nothing is familiar. She hesitates: " . . . surely she had come too far? This is not possible, she thought, this cannot be; surely our house was white? The evening was very dark, and she could see only the houses going in rows, with more rows beyond them and more beyond that, and somewhere a house which was hers, with the beautiful stranger inside, and she lost out here."[2] Thus the story ends with Margaret in a state of confusion. One realizes then that her previous anxiety has caused her mind to play tricks on her, as it has in the past two days; now she can no longer control its behavior or focus her wandering attention. Familiar objects are no longer meaningful; and, since she has lost touch with reality, she is, indeed, lost.

In the story "Island," one is told immediately that Mrs. Montague has "lost her mind." The opening lines read: "Mrs. Montague's son had been very good to her, with the kind affection and attention to her well-being that is seldom found toward mothers in sons with busy wives and growing families of their own; when Mrs. Montague lost her mind, her son came into his natural role of guardian. There had always been a great deal of warm feeling between Mrs. Montague and her son, and although they lived nearly a thousand miles apart by now, Henry Paul Montague was careful to see that his mother was well taken care of; . . ."[3]

From the point of view of society, wealthy Mrs. Montague is an invalid; this condition relegates her to confinement in her handsome apartment with a constant nurse-companion. While Henry Paul is described as a devoted son — for he is careful to supply money for all her needs, to pay the bills promptly, and to send weekly tender letters in longhand inquiring about her health — he comes to visit his mother only on rare trips to New York. Her physical needs, therefore, receive considerable attention while her emotional ones do not. Separated from the one person she loves, she has had, instead, for six years, Polly Oakes, a firm, rigid, insignificant individual who occupies herself by reading magazines, knitting, and studying the daily menu. Miss Oakes is kind to Mrs. Montague, but she becomes understandably exasperated when the elderly lady spills oatmeal on her beautiful dresses, refuses to eat, or tries to run away during the spells of restlessness that overcome her every year in late spring.

Except for one glimpse into the liberated spirit and dreams of Mrs. Montague, one sees events and objects as they appear to Miss Oakes, who is impressed with the thick, luxurious carpet; the silken curtains; the lovely clothes sent by the exclusive dress shop for Mrs. Montague's selection (her own clothes are garish reds and yellows, since the white uniforms seem to upset the old lady). She admires Mrs. Montague's shiny dark mink, the rich appointments of the apartment hotel, and especially the gourmet restaurant below from which she orders their meals. Eating has become the major preoccupation, a daily ritual that begins with careful devotion to an elaborate menu and ends with the offering up of the repast by hotel personnel and the religious consumption marred only by Mrs. Montague's mishaps. While Miss Oakes partakes of exotic foods, Mrs. Montague's fare is always oatmeal with pudding for dessert and sometimes, if she is good, ice cream.

One soon begins to pity the old woman, for she seems to yearn for color and beauty and for a wild outdoor freedom. In the apartment, she spends much time with crayons and a simple coloring book. Blue is her favorite; she loves the blue sky, blue water, a softly curved blue bowl she had seen in a shop window; and she paints everything blue. "Why look at you," Miss Oakes says. "You've gone and made the whole thing blue, you silly child." Mrs. Montague violently covers the picture. "Mine," she says. "Get away, this is mine." Later she says to her companion, "You don't know what things *are*, really." The materialistic Polly lacks the sensitivity to understand the loneliness and the hidden yearnings of the older woman. Every day on their walks Mrs. Montague pauses at the same shop windows, sometimes to admire the blue bowl, or some tea cakes, or a red and yellow plastic bird dipping its beak mechanically into a glass of water. "Pretty," she whispers, "pretty, pretty."

Without warning, the viewpoint changes, and the reader discovers the old lady's dreams. She is on an island: "She opened her eyes suddenly and was aware that she saw. The sky was unbelievably, steadily blue, and the sand beneath her feet was hot; she could see the water, colored more deeply than the sky, but faintly greener. Far off was the line where the sky and water met, and it was infinitely pure."[4] In her world of fantasy, following an impulse, she discards and then buries her clothing: fur coat, hat, shoes — all. Then, exulting in her freedom, she runs wildly across the sand; in a grove of nearby trees, she hears a parrot calling her. "Eat, eat," it shrieks, "eat, eat." For a moment the unpleasant idea of food comes to her, and she runs on; but later among the trees she sees and again hears the parrot, a "saw-toothed voice and a flash of ugly red and yellow." When she sits down a moment later in the cool grass by a little brook to eat, she has by her side "a shimmering glass . . . of dark red wine, a blue plate of soft chocolate cakes filled with cream"; and there are pomegranates, cheese, and "small sharp-flavored candies" — all of the delicacies she yearns for, but never receives in the prison of her sheltered, prosaic life.

Somewhere overhead, the parrot continues to scream; and she puts out a bit of cake for him. He hesitantly comes to feed, nibbling cautiously, lifting his beak, then lowering his head and lifting it again. The movement — which she has observed in the shop window

— seems familiar to her, but she does not know why. The parrot, one realizes, is the insistent Miss Oakes, who, afraid of the hot sand and the water, stays always in the trees "near the food." The dream sequence ends as abruptly as it began; in Miss Jackson's fiction, there is often no clear-cut distinction between the dream world and the real world, and the disturbed personality slips easily between the two. The reader has rather more difficulty; and, if for this reason alone, one must read the stories carefully and thoughtfully, and examine the subtleties of character, plot, and symbolism.

As the dream ends and one no longer shares Mrs. Montague's thoughts, the two ladies turn the corner and are almost home; back in their apartment, Miss Oakes orders their food, beginning with a martini for herself, prune juice for the old lady, and her usual oatmeal. And, while the younger woman busies herself with the ritual of the dinner menu, Mrs. Montague bends over her coloring book, busily at work on a farmyard scene — hens, a barn, trees, which she colors blue. With sudden inspiration she places a red and yellow blob in one of her blue trees, an outward sign of rebellion perhaps, but also one of inner satisfaction as she quietly puts Polly Oakes in her place.

As the blue suggests to her the freedom of the sky and the sea, the island of her dreams is a haven, far from the repressions she does not understand, where she can behave as her spirit pleases. Mrs. Montague is another of the confused, lonely persons that one finds in the fiction of Miss Jackson and for whom she shows sympathy. The Polly Oakeses, lacking sensitivity and therefore unresponsive to the needs of others, are the villains.

Loss of direction nevertheless may stem from many sources. An overdose of pain-deadening drugs is responsible for Clara Spencer's mental confusion in the story "The Tooth" (1950). One assumes her condition to be temporary, although the story ends with Clara's having forgotten her identity and with her running barefooted through the streets of New York, hand in hand with an imaginary man. Both Clara Spencer and Mrs. Montague ("The Island") yield to an urge to recover the natural freedom of youth.

II *Fantasy*

The stories of the psychologically confused are related, in a sense, to Miss Jackson's tales of fantasy; but it is difficult sometimes to make a clear-cut distinction between them since both contain believable characters and abound in authentic detail of an ordinary environment. For the reader, both may pose a problem in character identification, to which there may be any one of three possible solutions: (1) the character may be of a spiritual nature, such as a ghost — daytime or nighttime; (2) he may be the product of another character's imagination; (3) or he may be, after all, an ordinary flesh-and-blood person — but the reader often cannot be sure which of these interpretations is intended. As a result, one comes away from such stories or novels (*Hangsaman* or *The Haunting of Hill House*) with a frustrated pleasure — not quite understanding what has taken place, but enjoying the adventure all the same. For example, in many of the reviews of *Hangsaman*, critics interpreted the character of Tony as a product of Natalie's imagination; other reviewers treated Tony as a real girl (a Lesbian, one critic calls her).

"The Daemon Lover" (1949) has, in the person of James Harris, a character who might qualify for any one of the previous interpretations. An old ballad, "The Demon Lover," popular in England, Scotland, Ireland, and America, apparently served as the inspiration for the title of the story; but the resulting tale (which first appeared in the *Woman's Home Companion* in February, 1949, as "The Phantom Lover") bears little resemblance to the story of the ballad. In the Scottish version of the ballad, a seaman, James Harris, the demon lover, is thought to be dead; but he returns after seven years to claim his love who has, in the meantime, married and become the mother of two children. Persuading her to run away with him, he resumes his true character after they are at sea; and she discovers his "cloven foot" and realizes then that he is the devil and that they are going to the distant dreary frosty mountain he says is hell. Thereupon he breaks the ship in two and sinks it.

Shirley Jackson published two versions of the story. In the earlier one, "The Phantom Lover," James Harris appears to be an actual man who jilts his sweetheart on their wedding day; in the revised version, which is narrated from the point of view of the thirty-four-year-old heroine, the reader has cause to suspect that Harris may be either a product of her imagination or a phantom appearing momentarily to plague his victims and then disappear. The time is the wedding day; and, long after the hour when he was to appear at her apartment, she (one never learns her name) goes in search of him. Having known him only one month, she has never seen his apartment. She fails to find him at the address he has given her; and the superintendent tells her that no one by that name lives there, but his wife remembers that one of the families has lent an apartment to a young man for the past month and suggests that she inquire there.

The frustrated heroine asks, but receives no satisfaction from the tenants since the young man apparently had left that morning before they arrived — and, no, they did not really know him, having met him only once. She leaves the apartment building in despair but stops along the way at a delicatessen, a florist shop, a newsstand, to inquire about a young man who usually wears a blue suit. The florist acknowledges that a young man had come in to buy flowers that morning — chrysanthemums — but has no other information. Finally, several streets beyond, from a man selling shoelaces and from a boy standing nearby, she is directed into a small apartment house; the boy says he followed a man in a blue suit carrying flowers to the third floor as he wanted the man to give him a quarter. There are no names on the mailboxes, but she climbs the narrow, dirty stairs to the third floor, which has only two apartments, one of which, apparently used for storage, is empty. She knocks on the door of the other apartment and thinks that she hears voices, but suddenly everything is silent. She knocks again, but there is no answer. (In the earlier version, she recognizes Harris's voice in an apartment with another woman, and decides to leave.) Here, there is only silence. Miss Jackson has cleverly built suspense through the complicated search so that the reader is almost as anxious as the unfortunate lady to discover what is behind that closed door.

The final lines of the story read: "She knew there was someone inside the apartment, because she was sure she could hear low voices and sometimes laughter. She came back many times, every day for the first week. She came on her way to work, in the mornings; in the evenings, on her way to dinner alone, but no matter how often or how firmly she knocked, no one ever came to the door."[5] The reader may conclude whatever he pleases, but the indications are that James Harris is indeed a demonic creature. Appearing and disappearing at will, he attains satisfaction from pursuing and promising to marry frustrated, thirtyish females. The fact that no one ever seems to be in the apartment seems to preclude the theory that he is human, if indeed this place is his home. The tantalizing possibility remains — that the incident of the courtship and the character of Harris are a product of the lady's anxious imagination; for the reader has never met him; no one seems to know him or — considering the many young men who might be wearing blue suits — has ever seen him.

III *Ghosts*

Miss Jackson is an expert at summoning spirits for a full-fledged fantasy. For this type of story of suspense and terror she has gained a reputation (wrongly) of being a proponent of witches and witchcraft. She was fascinated by the supernatural, and there are ghosts in her fiction. But one finds in her tales no witches or vampires; no scenes in the graveyard at midnight and no villagers in the dark forest cavorting with evil spirits or Satan's henchmen — such as one finds in Hawthorne — no curses or spells; and no witchlike characters. Indeed, her story "The Witch" deals not with the supernatural but with a man's underlying evil nature.

Just as Hawthorne manages to blend the fantastic with the commonplace, so does Miss Jackson, with the exception that she deals with the present-day commonplace, relying upon convincing detail to gain acceptance for her characters and their "normal" environment. "The Visit" (1950), which contains supernatural elements in the appearance of ghosts who have assumed a modern form, is such a story. The physical description of the impressive house, its rooms, and its grounds furnishes the details that make the setting plausible and commonplace. The story begins with a description: "The house in itself was, even before anything had happened there, as lovely a thing as she had ever seen. Set among its lavish grounds, with a park and a river and a wooded hill surrounding it, and carefully planned and tended gardens close upon all sides, it lay upon the hills as though it were something too precious to be seen by everyone."[6]

The house is "lovely," and the surroundings have natural charm. The parklike setting with the river and the wooded hills suggests peace and tranquillity — certainly not a scene for ghostly characters, even the pleasant daylight variety. But this house, too, has its own little world. Protected by carefully planned gardens that surround it on all sides, the house itself, the author suggests, is meant to be seen only by the sensitive, the true lovers of beauty. The many rooms of the interior, colorful and cheerful, provide a believable but unusual background for a ghost story with a simple plot. During a summer vacation, Margaret visits her friend Carla at her family's expansive country estate where she meets several persons, all apparently relatives of Carla's family. The reader senses the strangeness that Margaret feels in the behavior of two of the members. At story's end — in a surprise twist — Margaret discovers that the two have been visible only to her and that they are permanent, charming ghosts who refuse to vacate the premises simply because they are dead.

The fantasy tale often exists for its own sake — for the pleasure and surprise it introduces, suggesting an enlargement of life in the form of a fourth dimension. Such a fantasy leads the reader to admit that his mind, after all, comprehends very little of what may be the completeness of experience. Another fantasy, "The Rock" (the symbolism of which is discussed later), involves three people who journey out of season to an island resort. Paula Ellison, with her convalescent brother and dependent sister-in-law, finds the rocklike island as disturbing as the only other guest, an insignificant-looking man who turns out to be Death. Death has come originally for the sister-in-law, but it chooses Paula instead.

Another, later story incorporating live ghosts is the story "Home," which, never anthologized, appeared in the *Ladies' Home Journal* of August, 1965, the month and year in which Shirley Jackson died. In this story, a young new-to-the-country wife on a rainy day picks up two hitchhikers, an old lady and a young boy. When they suddenly disappear from her car, she tells her writer-husband of the strange event and discovers that there is a legend that, sixty years before, a boy, living in their present house, had been stolen by an old woman; then both had been drowned when a nearby bridge was flooded. On the next day, also a rainy one, she realizes from an icy chill that the two ghosts are still in the car and that they intend her harm; for, as she nears the bridge, the car skids and is almost out of control. She manages to save herself while the ghosts, laughing wildly, disappear.

These tales are meant to amuse, to entertain the reader, by terror and suspense, although Miss Jackson seems to believe that certain manifestations are very real and that it is a mistake to think that one can laugh them out of "existence." Whether she acknowledged the presence of daylight ghosts is questionable, but she was aware of testimony regarding such visitations. In any case, she appreciated the chills and thrills of a good ghost story and knew that her readers did also. Suspense and terror, in whatever form, with or without ghosts are good ingredients for a short story; and, as one has seen, the sensitive, unhinged mind is especially prone to terrorization and can create its own nightmares.

A story of fear, perhaps one closely related to "The Tooth," is that of "The Bus" (1965). In both stories, the protagonists, or "victims," are under the influence of drugs: the first lady has tried to deaden the pain of her aching tooth; the second has taken a sleeping pill so that she may more comfortably endure an annoying bus trip. Old Miss Harper, a not-too-gracious lady, loathes the dirty, smelly bus she is forced to use and the irritating people with whom she is forced to come in contact. Having fallen asleep on the bus, she is abruptly awakened by the driver, who tells her that he is no alarm clock and that, since this is her stop, she must get off. The cross old lady intends to report the driver, as she tells him; then, struggling with her suitcase, she gets off, finding herself at an isolated road-crossing entitled Rickett's Landing. It is a dark rainy night, and never having seen this place before, she is lost. No lights or houses are visible. Fighting panic, she begins walking. A small truck comes by, and two young men reluctantly take the old lady in.

There is something ominous about the two; and, when the old lady makes disparaging remarks about the bus driver and says she will report him, the men, who know the driver, refuse to move. When Mrs. Harper quickly gets the message and promises not to report him, they drive her to a nearby roadhouse. At first, she is hesitant to go in; but she has no other choice. As she notices the once-lovely old house, now converted into a bar and grill, she realizes with a sense of pleasure that this house is very like her childhood home.

Inside, the people are objectionable and frightening, but she obtains a room for an exorbitant price. Upstairs, the feeling of familiarity with the house grows; but her terror increases when she imagines that she is a child again and that her once-loved toys in the closet suddenly come to life and rebel against her. The noise in the closet becomes unbearable; and, as she flees down the hall into the darkness, she calls for her mother. At that moment she hears the voice of the bus driver telling her that he is not an alarm clock and that she must get off the bus. The story ends as she again finds herself in the driving rain under the sign Rickett's Landing. The surprise ending reinforces the nightmarish quality of the experience.

Terror, frustration, and helplessness plague the heroine-victims of this type of story. Miss Jackson's skill in characterization is apparent in such persons as old Mrs. Harper, who is not an entirely sympathetic character; in fact, she is cross, critical of others, narrow-minded, and selfish. She finds fault with the bus; she is annoyed by the other passengers; she is furious with the driver who is only doing his job. Of course, he is the one who mistakes the stop; but then, as far as the reader knows, perhaps his action is also a part of her unpleasant dream. Mrs. Harper's age and her helplessness keep her a sympathetic character. At the end of the story, one pities her. But where does the dream end and the reality begin? Again, the reader must decide for himself; but he will never know for sure.

IV   *Suspense And Terror*

Less often in the tales of suspense, the terror stems from fear of harm from actual people. In the nonfantasy stories, the source of fear has been psychological; and, while it is very real to the individual, the reader is aware that outside forces have not threatened to destroy the principals. The main characters of "The Summer People" (chosen for *Best American Short Stories, 1951*) and "The Little House" (1960), however, feel threatened by outsiders. Miss Jackson cleverly draws a veil over the threatening agents, whom one never sees, although definite signs seem to indicate their presence. Again, the question of what is real and what is imagined arises. At the end of the stories, the victims are waiting, lonely and helpless; the situation has not been resolved; and the reader is left in suspense.

Elderly Janet Allison and her husband in "The Summer People" decide to remain at the lonely lake cottage after the end of the season instead of returning to the city. On their biweekly visit to the village to purchase supplies, they inform the various shopkeepers that they will be staying on for another month. All seem surprised; nobody, they say, stays after the season. From Mrs. Allison's critical view, one sees the staunch storekeepers as somewhat less than bright and, as she later discovers, not excessively honest. Immediately, little cracks appear in the facade of the Allisons' comfortable existence: the weekly letters from their son and daughter are late; their cottage has none of the modern conveniences; the oil supply for the stove and lamps will last one more day, but the regular driver cannot furnish them oil since he had ordered only enough for the summer months; the grocer can no longer deliver supplies in their area as his summer delivery boy is now back in school; and the John Halls, their nearest neighbors (three miles away), who bring them butter and eggs, are gone, visiting her parents upstate. And yet, strangely, there had been lights at the Hall place the night before.

The Allisons gradually become aware of their increasing isolation from the community in a situation they find at first merely irritating but soon perilous; for Mr. Allison discovers that their car will not start; and, as he later tells Mrs. Allison, "The car had been tampered with, you know. Even I could see that." The long-awaited letter from the son arrives with the envelope suspiciously smudged by fingerprints and with the message that, as long as they enjoy the country so much, they should stay at the lake cottage for another month. The final blow comes when they attempt to call the garage about the car and find the phone dead. "I suppose the phone wires were cut," she says afterward as they sit quietly in the flickering shadow of the kerosene lamp, waiting for whatever is to happen.

Again Miss Jackson allows events to transpire in such a plausible manner that the reader is uneasily aware that the occurrences may have been due to coincidence and that the elderly couple may have become victims of their own groundless fears. But the evidence seems sufficient to urge one to share the suspicion that foul play, not from spirits but from flesh-and-blood villains, is intended. Whatever the cause, the reader is left in suspense to wonder at and fear for the Allisons' safety.

In another story of the same type, "The Little House" (1960), a young city woman has inherited an elderly aunt's house in the country. Happily intending to make this her first real home, she plans removing all the unnecessary bric-a-brac, such as the moose head in the hall, and filling the house with bright colors. The house, like that of "The Summer People," is ill lighted and full of shadows. In the evening, as she moves from room to room making plans and at the same time speculating as to where her aunt was found after her fatal heart attack, two fussy old neighbor ladies come for an informal visit. It is soon evident that neither Miss Amanda nor Miss Caroline approves of a city lady taking over "Aunt's" possessions. (As one sees, in Miss Jackson's stories city people are often the victims of prejudice and oppression on the part of the natives.)

Miss Caroline persists in remarks that Miss Amanda labels as "gossip" and "wild stories" but that suggest that an intruder found his way through the broken kitchen door and murdered the old lady. Two months have apparently passed since her death, and no accusations have been made; but, as they leave, Miss Caroline warns the niece to keep the kitchen door locked, for he might come back. When the ladies leave and the niece is left alone in the semidarkness, she imagines the intruder creeping up behind her aunt — or did he waylay her on the dark stairs? As she climbs the stairs, feeling for the knob of the bedroom door, she suddenly panics, wondering who or what is waiting behind the door; and she runs wildly back to the lighted kitchen. Meanwhile, Miss Amanda and Miss Caroline sit contentedly at home drinking tea, criticizing the newcomer for usurping "Aunt's" valuables, and speculating about her desirability as a neighbor. Miss Caroline says — and one may suspect her of malicious intent — "She might not like it here. . . . Perhaps she won't stay." The niece's peace of mind has been destroyed, but was the evil intentional?

Many of Miss Jackson's righteous old ladies are inherently evil and deliberately malicious. And, even though Miss Caroline's sin may be confined to innocent gossip, she has successfully destroyed another's peace of mind. Is there an intruder waiting in the darkness? Was the aunt murdered? These questions are not answered, but there is the possibility of deliberate cruelty on the part of the insider who will not easily accept the outsider. Beneath the seemingly gentle exterior, ugliness exists. This theme of reality versus appearance, or of evil cloaked in seeming good, is the theme of another group of stories, in each of which mankind is exposed as basically evil.

V *Evil Beneath a Mild Exterior*

What evil lurks within the hearts of men — and old women? In addition to those mentioned previously in "The Little House," there are three notable examples of grandmotherly types who differ from the popular image of goodness, grace, and charm. Each of the older ladies in "Trial by Combat," "Whistler's Grandmother," and "Possibility of Evil" is intent on mischief. The least harmful, yet a rather sinister character — because she seems to have no conscience — is Mrs. Archer in "Trial by Combat," a respectable old lady who unashamedly steals from the other inhabitants of her rooming house.

The "sweet" old grandmother in "Whistler's Grandmother" (1945) is on her way to New York City to warn her returning soldier-grandson that his city wife has been receiving strange letters from men. She loves her grandson but cannot tolerate his pretty wife; therefore, she is about to expose her for nonexistent crimes. Obviously irony is an important ingredient in each of these stories, for the reader sees these old women in quite a different way from that in which they see themselves and from which society views them. Whistler's Grandmother, a hypocrite, is intent on injuring an innocent human being. The story's title emphasizes the contrast between the outward show of goodness and gentleness and the ugliness within.

In 1965, Miss Jackson was still pursuing the wicked old lady theme; and perhaps the most malicious of her characters of this type is Miss Adela Strangeworth in "The Possibility of Evil," her last short story which appeared in the December 18, 1965, issue of *The Saturday Evening Post*, four months after Miss Jackson's death. Seventy-one-year-old Miss Strangeworth, the last of a well-known and respected family, decides that there is too much evil in the world, especially in "her" town. To correct this situation and to warn others of evil, she, ironically becomes evil. She writes short, cryptic — poison-pen — notes in penciled block letters to various people in town, and secretly mails them at night. "Miss Strangeworth never concerned herself with facts; her letters all dealt with the more negotiable stuff of suspicion." Completely hypocritical, she is outwardly friendly to the same people she secretly attacks. To the young couple, concerned with the seemingly slow progress of their six-month-old baby, she writes: "DIDN'T YOU EVER SEE AN IDIOT CHILD BEFORE? SOME PEOPLE JUST SHOULDN'T HAVE CHILDREN, SHOULD THEY?" To Mrs. Harper, to whom she has written previously and who, she decides, looks rather shaky, she writes: "HAVE YOU FOUND OUT YET WHAT THEY WERE ALL LAUGHING ABOUT AFTER YOU LEFT THE BRIDGE CLUB ON THURSDAY? OR IS THE WIFE REALLY ALWAYS THE LAST ONE TO KNOW?"

In contrast, the poor, hard-working people surrounding Miss Strangeworth seem harried and guiltless; but she insidiously destroys their peace of mind until she accidentally drops a letter one night. Again, with a stroke of irony, one of the past victims sees her; but, unknowingly and out of kindness, the finder delivers the dropped letter to the intended victim. Miss Strangeworth awakens the next morning with "a feeling of intense happiness" at the thought of the letters sent the night before until, among the mail on the hall floor, she finds and opens a poison-pen letter addressed to her. She has been discovered. She begins to cry silently for "the wickedness of the world" as she reads: "LOOK OUT AT WHAT USED TO BE YOUR ROSES." Her beautiful roses have always been her most prized possession, a fact Miss Jackson has carefully developed. And they have now been destroyed in retaliation for her wickedness, but it is characteristic of these ladies not to recognize their own evil. It is not they who are at fault, but the rest of the world — the final irony.

But not all of the perpetrators of evil are female; some males, who are also not what they seem, have a polite, smiling exterior that hides their ugliness within. Sometimes Miss Jackson uses this revelation as the special twist at the end of the story. In one of the earlier *New Yorker* stories, "On the House" (1943), a blind man and his supposed bride come into a liquor store to buy supplies to celebrate their wedding. Artie, at the counter, offers to give them either scotch (which the man wants) or brandy (which she favors) at a discount as a wedding present. After they choose the brandy, the better buy, the blind man produces four bills since the price is four dollars; however, he presents a five and three singles. Not wishing to embarrass the man, Artie quietly calls this to the wife's attention. She states proudly that her husband knows one bill from another, and then silently takes the change as Artie gives it to her.

A few minutes later, the blind man returns with his wife and loudly proclaims that he has been cheated. He says that he realizes now that he had handed Artie a five and three singles. Artie, acknowledging this, says he gave the change to the wife. The wife denies it and threatens to call the police. Artie, who knows when he has been taken, produces four more dollars, which the man pockets, and then, putting the brandy under his arm, he and she leave. Through this cunning ruse, they have acquired a $4.97 bottle of brandy for nothing. The irony lies in the reversal of expectation: the blind man has used his affliction and the resulting sympathy to defraud an unsuspecting, and, momentarily, kindhearted individual.

Another unusual story with the same theme and with a twist is "One Ordinary Day With Peanuts" — selected for *Best American Short Stories, 1956* and first published in *Fantasy and Science Fiction Magazine*. In this story, Mr. John Philip Johnson leaves his house in the morning armed with candy and peanuts. Throughout the day, he seeks opportunities to perform kind acts and, in the process, gives away not only peanuts but money. At the end of the day, coinciding with the end of the story, he comes home to his wife, who has spent the day performing evil deeds: accusing an innocent lady of shoplifting; sending three dogs to the pound, etc. Mr. Johnson applauds her fine efforts and then suggests that they *trade* tomorrow, implying that he will then be the wicked one and she the distributor of good. The reader suddenly realizes that this standard exchange is the way in which Mr. and Mrs. Johnson get their enjoyment: by taking turns at playing God and Satan. For the reader, the ultimate horror of the situation lies in the lack of conscience of the two and in their utter disregard for right and wrong as they interfere with the lives of others for sport. But Miss Jackson's characters are not "heavies"; she treats them lightly so that the revelation, despite its seriousness, becomes funny. Again, one sees evidence of Miss Jackson the entertainer.

There are other stories in which young people are the victims of either thoughtlessness or malicious intent: for instance, one has the ill treatment of a young girl whose parents have been killed in an accident, and who has been taken in by a hypocritical neighbor, in the story "All She Said Was Yes" (1962); and the injury to the teen-age boy by the man he aided in "Seven Types of Ambiguity" (1948). But

such cruelty also extends into the animal world; and the most pleasant, harmless-looking people can expose the ugliness of their
natures in their treatment of less fortunate creatures.

In the story "The Renegade" (1948), for example, the victim is a
dog belonging to the Walpoles who have recently moved from the
city to a country community. Lady Walpole, a gentle and lovable
family pet, has suddenly killed, but not eaten, three of the
neighbor's chickens; and everyone asks Mrs. Walpole what they are
going to do about the dog. Once a chicken-killer, they say, always a
chicken-killer. Kindhearted Mrs. Walpole is shaken by the "cures"
suggested. Through the use of the outsider and her reactions to the
advice given, Miss Jackson gives the reader a horrifying glimpse of
man's innate cruelty. The more humane persons advise chaining or
shooting the dog. Old Mr. White proposes that they tie a dead
chicken around the dog's neck until it rots and falls off by itself. The
grocer then recalls his father's cure for an egg-eating dog:

So he took an egg once, set it on the back of the stove for two, three days, till
the egg got good and ripe, good and hot through and that egg smelled pretty
bad. Then — I was there, boy twelve, thirteen years old — he called the dog
one day, and the dog come running. So I held the dog, and my daddy
opened the dog's mouth and put the egg, red-hot and smelling to heaven,
and then he held the dog's mouth closed so's the dog couldn't get rid of the
egg any way except to swallow.[7]

To the grocer's comment that thereafter the dog would run when he
saw an egg, Mrs. Walpole asks, "But how did he feel about you? . . .
Did he ever come near *you* again?" The grocer seems surprised, as
though the question were irrelevant, but then he says, "No, . . . I
don't believe you could say's he ever did. Not much of a dog,
though."[8]

Another man says she should take her dog "and put him in a pen
with a mother hen's got chicks to protect." When asked what would
happen, he replies, "Scratch his eyes out. . . . He wouldn't ever be
able to *see* another chicken." Understandably upset, Mrs. Walpole
leaves the store. Even at home, when the children arrive from
school, she discovers that they, too, can discuss the possible tortures
without visible emotion. A Mr. Shepherd, a genial man who gives
the children nickels and takes the boys fishing, had told them that
they could get a collar for the dog in which they were to hammer
spikes, attach it to a long rope, and pull the rope when the dog

chases a chicken. "And," says her son Jack, "the spikes cut her head off."[9] As the children laugh, Mrs. Walpole stares at them in amazement, and retreats then to the out-of-doors to get a breath of fresh air, to be reassured by the peaceful landscape: the sunny sky and the gentle line of the hills.

The children, perhaps, are not aware of the significance of their chatter; moreover, the hypothetical situation is not real to them, although they are delighted with its possibilites. They love their dog; but Mrs. Walpole realizes, nevertheless, as Miss Jackson obviously does, that children are not immune to the latent cruelties that sprout in adults. They, too, contain their share of the evil that is the lot of mankind. Miss Jackson, one presumes, believes that man has a choice; he need not be evil, and it behooves him to fight these tendencies toward evil, not only in himself, but in others. None of the stories — except the comic ones — has a happy ending. The dilemmas remain unresolved, as does the problem with Lady Walpole in this story. The situation is presented; and the lesson, if any, comes from the reader's exposure to the evil and from the insights he gains therefrom.

VI *Prejudice*

Social prejudice, another by-product of man's inclination toward hypocrisy and cruelty, is also an important subject in Miss Jackson's fiction: prejudice against Negroes, against Jews, against city people in a country community. In her own life, newly arrived from San Francisco, she had experienced the snobbishness of cliques at Brighton High School in Rochester; she was the outsider who did not quite fit in; and her situation was very much the same during her year at the University of Rochester, which many of the girls from the city's old families attended. As Mrs. Stanley Edgar Hyman, she learned about anti-Semitic prejudices; but she had already been aware of hostile feelings toward isolated Jewish families during the early days in Burlingame, California; and as a city person in a Vermont country town she again knew what it was to be an outsider. On the other hand, in 1939, she had actively campaigned for racial integration of the college dormitories at Syracuse University; and in Vermont she publicly denounced the annual blackface theatricals sponsored by the local Lions Club. She had a keen sense of justice, which is evident in her literary work.

Two of the early *New Yorker* stories deal with prejudice: "A Fine Old Firm" (1944) contains hints of anti-Semitism, and "After You,

My Dear Alphonse" (1943) concerns erroneous conceptions about
Negro people. In this last story, Mrs. Wilson exhibits the stock
response of many whites toward Negro families. She is a bit surprised when her young son Johnny brings home Boyd, a little Negro
boy, for lunch. As they eat, she questions Boyd in a patronizing way;
and in her doing so, one sees her image of the typical Negro family;
when his responses do not fit her preconceived notions, she is upset.
Boyd's father does work in a factory, but he isn't big and strong, and
he doesn't spend his time lifting and carrying; he is a foreman. In
answer to Mrs. Wilson's questions as to what his mother does, Boyd
says, "She takes care of us kids." She discovers also that the family is
not large; Boyd has only one sister, Jean, who is going to be a
teacher.

She urges Boyd to take his fill of food; and then, thinking to be
kind, she suggests giving him some of Johnny's suits that are now too
small and also a few of her own dresses that his mother and sister
might wear or remake. He should, in fact, take home a bundle right
away, but Boyd says: "But I have plenty of clothes, thank you. . . .
And I don't think my mother knows how to sew very well, and
anyway I guess we buy about everything we need. Thank you very
much, though."[10] Annoyed, Mrs. Wilson lifts the plate of ginger-
bread off the table just as Boyd is about to take another piece. She is
angry with him for being "ungrateful"; and, sensing this reaction,
he apologizes: "I didn't mean to make you mad, Mrs. Wilson." Then
the boys go off together; their own relationship is one of sharing — a
give-and-take common ground, "after you, my dear Alphonse."
Mrs. Wilson, on the other hand, may never learn about the violation
of dignity.

VII *The Lonely Career Girl*

In the 1940's when Miss Jackson herself was a New Yorker, she
wrote of the loneliness and frustration of the out-of-town career girl
who makes the city her home. As the years pass, the dreams of
glamour and success fade; and the heroine becomes unlovely, lonely,
and selfish. Three notable stories in this group are "The Villager"
(1944), "I Know Who I Love" (1946), and "Elizabeth" (1949). For
example, Hilda Clarence ("The Villager"), now thirty-five years old,
had come to Greenwich Village twelve years before to be a dancer;
but, being practical and having taken a course in shorthand and typing, she has become a secretary. Now, answering an advertisement
about the sale of some furniture, she visits the apartment of a young

couple who are moving to Paris: she is a dancer; he, an artist. Alone in their rather shabby apartment, Hilda briefly relives some of her dreams and ambitions and then leaves, a bit sadder and a bit more lonely.

Another of these sad ladies is Elizabeth Style ("Elizabeth"), who has been working for the past eleven years with a second-rate literary agent who has come to depend upon her. She manipulates him and others to serve her own ends and then deserts him for someone who can help her more. Such girls adjust to a life that has become a series of disappointments, but they are not yet ready to recognize themselves as failures.

VIII *Social Evil* — *"The Lottery"*

One of the ancient practices that modern man deplores as in-humanly evil is the annual sacrifice of a scapegoat or a god-figure for the benefit of the community. Throughout the ages, from ancient Rome and Greece to the more recent occurrences in African coun-tries, sacrifices in the name of a god of vegetation were usual and necessary, the natives felt, for a fertile crop. Somewhere along the way, the sacrifice of a human for the sins of the people — to drive evil from themselves — became linked with the ritual of the vegeta-tion god. In Mexico, among the Aztecs, the victims impersonated the particular gods for a one-year period before being put to death; death came then by the thrust of a knife into the breast and the im-mediate extraction of the heart. In Athens, each year in May, at the festival of the Thargelia, two victims, a man and a woman, were led out of the city and stoned to death.[11] Death by stoning was one of the accepted and more popular methods of dispatching ceremonial vic-tims.

But modern man considers such practices barbaric and, therefore, alien to his civilized behavior. For this reason, many persons were puzzled and shocked by "The Lottery." After its appearance in the June 28, 1948, issue of *The New Yorker*, a flood of mail — hundreds of letters — deluged both the editorial offices in New York and the post office in Bennington. No *New Yorker* story had ever received such a response. Of the many letters received, as Miss Jackson recalled, only thirteen spoke kindly to her; and those were from friends. Three main characteristics dominated the letters: bewilder-ment, speculation, and old-fashioned abuse. "The general tone of the early letters was a kind of wide-eyed shocked innocence. People at first were not so much concerned with what the story meant: what they wanted to know was where these lotteries were held, and whether they could go there and watch."[12] Later, after the story had been anthologized, televised, and dramatized, the tone of the letters became more polite; but people still wondered what the story meant.

She had conceived the story idea, she said, on a fine June morning as she was returning from a trip to the grocery store and was pushing uphill the stroller containing her daughter and the day's groceries. Having the idea well in mind, she wrote the story so easily that the finished copy was almost the same word for word as the rough draft. Her agent, she recalls, did not care for the story; nor was the fiction editor of *The New Yorker* particularly impressed; however, the magazine was going to buy it. When Mr. Harold Ross, then editor of the magazine, indicated that the story might be puzzling to some people and asked if she would care to enlarge upon its meaning, she refused. But later, in response to numerous requests, she made the following statement, which appeared in the July 22 issue of the *San Francisco Chronicle:* "Explaining just what I had hoped the story to say is very difficult. I suppose, I hoped, by setting a particularly brutal ancient rite in the present and in my own village to shock the story's readers with a graphic dramatization of the pointless violence and general inhumanity in their own lives."

Several of Miss Jackson's friends had intimated that the village characters were modeled after actual persons in Bennington; but, if so, she took pains to disguise the fact. The names are plain, solid-sounding: Adams, Warner, Dunbar, Martin, Hutchinson, etc. The name Mr. Summers is particularly suitable for sunny, jovial Joe Summers; it emphasizes the surface tone of the piece and underscores the ultimate irony. Mr. Graves — the postmaster and the assistant to Mr. Summers in the administration of the lottery — has a name that might well signify the tragic undercurrent, which does not become meaningful until the end of the story. As in the other stories designating the presence of evil even in the least likely persons, such as in sweet old ladies, the reader discovers the blight in this deceptively pleasant community. In fact, much of the horror stems from the discrepancy between the normal outward appearance of the village life and its people and the heinous act these people commit in the guise of tradition.

The story begins with a fine sunny morning, June 27 (the fiction editor had asked for a change in date, to coincide with this particular edition of *The New Yorker*). At first, the village appears to have a holiday atmosphere; and the reader's expectations are that the lottery is a joyous occasion, ending with a happy surprise for some lucky individual. The whole lottery, one is told, takes less than two hours, so that, if it begins at ten o'clock, the villagers will be home in time for noon dinner. Not until the truth of the lottery is revealed can the reader appreciate the chilling callousness of this business-as-usual attitude on the part of the community and the willingness of the people to accept and dismiss torture-death as a common occurrence. The gathering of the stones in one corner of the square is the part of the ceremony performed by the schoolchildren during their "boisterous play." The children, too, are guilty; they show no sensitivity or emotion about the coming event. Miss Jackson's matter-of-fact description is allied to the attitude of the townspeople, and this objectivity sustains the suspense and heightens the shock of the ending.

As the men congregate, they talk of "planting and rain, tractors and taxes." The women exchange bits of gossip. One notices the first bit of tension when the families gather together; the women, standing by their husbands, call to their children. Mr. Martin speaks sharply to Bobby when the boy runs back to the pile of stones, and Bobby comes quickly. As the black box is set down, the villagers keep their distance, leaving a space between themselves and the stool; and there is hesitation at Mr. Summers's call for assistance. But Miss Jackson so skillfully weaves the tension of the present with description of the past and with the history of the black box that the reader is kept carefully unaware of anything more than what, he supposes, is the normal excitement of the occasion.

Jovial Mr. Summers who, it would seem, is the epitome of civic duty, conducts the lotteries, as he also conducts the square dances, the teen-age club, and the Halloween program. The incongruity of the purpose and the seriousness of these four activities is ironic and testifies to the guilt in Mr. Summers's soul, for he is a willing leader and thus a perpetrator of the evil. His conscience is as blank as the — all but one — little slips in the little black box. He does not recognize evil or, perhaps, know right from wrong. He does not question the tradition of the lottery; instead, his token civic improvements call not for elimination of the lottery but for the substitution of slips of paper for chips of wood — for convenience and expediency.

Mr. Summers's cheerful mien belies the seriousness of the occasion. When Tessie has been chosen, and the fatal moment has come, it is Mr. Summers who says, "All right, folks. . . . Let's finish quickly." He shows no hesitation and no compassion. Because of his position in the community, he is the one who might successfully repudiate tradition; but he is representative of conservative elements who, though outwardly progressive, are content to retain existing though harmful customs. He is aware of the changing conditions in other villages; for, as Mr. and Mrs. Adams point out, some villages have already "quit lotteries." The Adamses are among the few progressive people who question the tradition and who implicitly suggest action, but their convictions are not strong; worse, they go along with the majority. Indeed, when the mob is upon Tessie, the hypocritical Steve Adams, ready to kill, is at the front of the group.

Old Man Warner, who miraculously has survived seventy-seven lotteries, is a frightening individual because, still completely superstitious, he wholeheartedly believes in the lottery and is convinced that the ritual is necessary for the welfare of the corn crop. He resents the amiable spirit and the jokes of Mr. Summers ("Bad enough to see young Joe Summers up there joking with everybody"), for he senses the seriousness of the occasion and the necessity of preserving the religiosity of the ceremony. It is not the death of the victim that disturbs him but the possible consequences of an irreligious attitude on the part of the participants. To Mr. Adams, he repeats the old saw: "Lottery in June, corn be heavy soon." Then he adds, after the comment on stopping the lottery, "First thing you know, we'd all be eating stewed chickweed and acorns" — if the lottery were to be abandoned, the crops would be destroyed and man would soon be foraging for food as he did in his cave-dwelling days. He does not want to go back to living in a cave, although in terms of civilization and humanity, he has never emerged from one, "There's *always* been a lottery," he says, and that alone, he supposes, is reason enough to continue the practice.

Tessie Hutchinson shows both the evils and the weaknesses of mankind faced with immediate death. Her hypocrisy indicates that she would willingly take part in the stoning; but, when she is the chosen sacrifice, she protests the unfairness of the method; she is not willing to be a good sport about giving up her life. "Be a good sport, Tessie," Mrs. Delacroix calls; and Mrs. Graves says, "All of us took the same chance." Instead, Tessie reacts like a frightened animal; but, unlike the animal-mother, the human mother does not always seek protection for her offspring. In fact, instead of giving her life for her children, Tessie prefers that they take their chances also — and she tries to have her daughter Eva and her husband Don included in the fatal drawing to increase her own chances for survival. The most pathetic figure of all is little Davy Hutchinson who survives the drawing but who is then forced, unknowing, to take part in the ordeal. Someone gives him a few pebbles so that he, too, may share in the collective murder of his mother; and his silence in this terrible moment is much more chilling than any other response Miss Jackson could have chosen for him.

If anything is illogical about the total ritual, it may be the stoicism of the participants and their complete willingness to sacrifice themselves or members of their families. As not all individuals are equally willing and able to endure pain, much less death, it would seem likely that during lottery time whole families might take to the woods or migrate to other villages. Even the Aztec god-figures, celebrated and worshipped until the sacrifice day, had to be guarded against escape. If the victim escaped, the captain of the guards became the substitute. But, since such practices are not literally a part of our culture, one may say that the story proceeds by way of realism to grimly realistic fantasy. As such, the lottery may be symbolic of any of a number of social ills that mankind blindly perpetrates.

IX *Short Story Collections*

In 1949 Farrar, Strauss published, as has been stated, a collection of Miss Jackson's short stories entitled *The Lottery, or The Adventures of James Harris* (an Avon paperback edition followed some years later in 1960). The James Harris figure, mentioned previously as derived from an old ballad, had no doubt been placed in several stories to provide some semblance of unity; however, none of the in-name-only Harris characters has any relationship or likeness to the others, and he is often only a minor character. The most famous of the Harris stories, "The Daemon Lover," is included in the collection, as are some of the best stories Miss Jackson ever wrote: "The Villager," "The Renegade," "Charles," "Flower Garden," "Dorothy and My Grandmother and the Sailors," "Elizabeth," "Seven Types of Ambiguity," "Come Dance With Me in Ireland," "Pillar of Salt," "The Tooth," and, of course, "The Lottery." As an epilogue to the stories, Miss Jackson presented the last seven stanzas of the Scottish version of the James Harris ballad (Child Ballad No. 243).

Another unifying device, criticized by some reviewers since it has no real bearing on the stories, is the inclusion of four passages from Joseph Glanvil's *Sadducismus Triumphatus* (a seventeenth-century defense of witchcraft) as dividers for the sections of the book. The motivation seems to have been an attempt by the publicity staff to make the book appear mysterious and, therefore, more salable. In a letter to her mother, Miss Jackson complained: " . . . The book is terrible. I read it a few days ago and it's flashy and sensational and all fixed up to sell. And every advance review we've seen is favorable although they keep referring to Saki, and Truman Capote, and John Collier, none of them writers I admire particularly, as people of whom the stories are reminiscent."[13]

Somehow Miss Jackson had already acquired a "witchlike" image, probably from well-meaning but misdirected publicity and from readers of "The Lottery" who tended to associate stoning with witches. Unfortunately, the promotion material only encouraged a false view of her and her writing, a view that may have added to popular interest but one that actually undermined her serious work. The reviews of the book were, as Miss Jackson indicated to her mother, generally favorable; and James Hilton in the May 1, 1949, issue of the *New York Herald Tribune Book Review* said of the stories that they "remind one of the elemental terrors of childhood. The whole collection will enhance Miss Jackson's reputation as a writer not quite like any other of her generation. Indeed she sees life in her own style, as devastatingly as Dali paints it, and like Dali also, she has a sound technique in her art."

Although Miss Jackson wrote many stories for individual magazines, this was to be the first and last collection of her stories published in her lifetime. In 1966, Stanley Edgar Hyman edited a posthumous anthology, *The Magic of Shirley Jackson*, containing eleven short stories and three complete books (*The Bird's Nest, Life Among the Savages,* and *Raising Demons*); by 1970, this book was in its third printing. Then again in 1968 Mr. Hyman edited the volume *Come Along With Me*, which contains as the title story the unfinished novel upon which Shirley Jackson was at work at the time of her death, as well as fourteen short stories, selected from about seventy-five not previously collected, which show the range and variety of her work over a thirty-year period. Also included in the book are three lectures that she had delivered at colleges and writers' conferences. The book itself had been dedicated, as Mr. Hyman said that she had wished it, to her good friend and agent, Carol Brandt.

X *Humorous Autobiographical Tales*

One cannot read Shirley Jackson's stories without marveling at her keen spirit of fun. Most of her humorous tales, based upon her own experiences as wife and mother, appeared first as magazine stories and then were later included in the two volumes *Life Among the*

Savages and *Raising Demons* (see Chapter 6). Although Miss Jackson and Mr. Hyman did not take them seriously, the stories sold well and were easy products of her flair for interpreting the comic aspects of daily living. She does not hesitate to poke fun at either her husband or herself, and both at times appear ridiculous and vulnerable when confronted with family problems. The four children from the baby to the eldest are ingenious and yet, in their adventures, typical of the children of ordinary families, although one cannot regard the Hymans as an ordinary family.

During the course of the tales, the children grow older; there are family moves, changes of cars, etc. — so that the finished collections are a biographical account covering, perhaps, a ten-year period. Miss Jackson presents the material with so much authority that the reader does not question its validity. And yet the author, as a true storyteller, has heightened the drama and added a few touches of color here and there. Throughout her work, one can see that Miss Jackson understands human nature and, amazingly, the minds of children. She is excellent with their dialogue. She also perceives the human element in animals and can, convincingly, make them appear cleverer than people.

In these humorous stories, her satire is gentle: she may stick pins into people, but she does not stab them. She makes use of the unexpected, and the incongruous, and often uses reversal of roles and situations. For instance, the notorious kindergartener about whom Laurie brings home stories (in "Charles") turns out to be Laurie himself. As in "Charles," some of the tales have surprise endings, but most of them depend upon a consistent pattern of humor. "The Night We All Had Grippe" is an excellent example, for in this story one sees Miss Jackson, the sad, overworked mother, attempting to care for her stricken household while she too is running a fever.

"My Son and the Bully," "The Third Baby Is The Easiest," "The Box," "Shopping Trip," etc., are all stories that appeared in various magazines, the majority in *Good Housekeeping* and in *Woman's Home Companion*. Because these stories are playful and seem slight, critics with no humor have been inclined to discount Miss Jackson's talents; and, consequently, her reputation as a writer may have suffered. But those who know her work consider the family chronicles another delightful aspect of Miss Jackson's genius.

XI *Characteristics of Style*

The diversity of the themes of the short stories indicates the range of Miss Jackson's interests. Even the themes of the four most anthologized stories — "The Lottery," "One Ordinary Day With Peanuts," "After You, My Dear Alphonse," and "Charles" — are quite different; they range from social evil and prejudice to the humorous family-incident tale. Since truth and simplicity are essential to her themes, she chooses to write in a plain, unadorned, straightforward manner. Her prose is poetic but not flowery, and she uses little figurative language and few metaphors or similes. For example, one sees this simplicity in a paragraph of "Come Along With Me" in which the narrator expresses satisfaction with the room she has rented: "I have a real feeling for shapes; I like things square, and my room was finely square. Even though I couldn't cook there I thought I could be happy. I wanted the barest rock bottom of a room I could have, I wanted nothing but a place to sleep and a place to sit and a place to put my things; any decorating done to my environment is me."[4]

The tone in this passage is conversational, almost intimate; the words are well-chosen, basic, short. Only two are more than two syllables in length. The repeated words "square" and "a place" give balance and a homely lyricism to the speaker's tone. Not unlike the author herself, the narrator in this case is an unusual middle-aged woman who, by choice, is completely alone for the first time in her life and is enjoying the adventure of shifting for herself in a strange environment. She abhors fuss and frills, finding beauty in plainness. In the same way, Miss Jackson in her language reveals an appreciation of the beauty of plainness of diction, one that matches her subject.

Again, one notes the simple but lyric quality of the following description of Mrs. Montague in "Island": "Finally she lay down and put her face to the sand. It was hot, hotter than anything else had ever been, and the soft grits of sand slipped into her mouth, where she could taste them, deliciously hard and grainy against her teeth; they were in her eyes, rich and warm; the sand was covering her face and the blue sky was gone from above her and the sand was cooler, then grayer, covering her face, and cold."[15]

The adjectives are sensory descriptions of the sun, the sky, the sand; and they involve sight, taste, and touch, and range in the one paragraph from hot to cold, soft to hard, blue to gray. The lone metaphor "the soft grits of sand," which are "grainy against her teeth" and "deliciously hard," extends the references to food made in earlier and later paragraphs of the story. The seven *and*s link the series of descriptive clauses, phrases, and sometimes single-word adjectives, thereby giving the lines a distinct poetic rhythm.

In general, her descriptions show no affectation, for she practices an economy of words, using homely adjectives sparingly: "rich and warm," or in other instances words such as "the small wind," "the sharp air," "the peeling wallpaper," "the sagging floor." Her colors are most often solid and undiluted: blues, reds, greens, yellows. She avoids the more feminine shades: beige, amber, aqua, burgundy, cerise, or turquoise. She says "the distant green hills"; "the half bushel of red eating apples"; " . . . the stirring of green life even under the dirty city traffic"; and, again, in "Island": "The sky was unbelievably, steadily blue, and the sand beneath her feet was hot; she could see the water colored more deeply than the sky, but faintly greener."[16]

The descriptions are literal rather than figurative; and, as they move the story forward, they tend to be purposeful rather than ornamental. For instance, in "The Visit," Carla greets Margaret, her house guest: "Carla stopped before the doorway and stood for a minute looking first behind her, at the vast reaching gardens and the green lawn going down to the river, and the soft hills beyond, and then at the perfect grace of the house, showing so clearly the long-boned structure within, the curving staircases and the arched doorways and the tall thin lines of steadying beams, all of it resting back against the hills, and up, past rows of windows and the flying lines of the roof, on to the tower — Carla stopped, and looked, and smiled, and then turned and said, 'Welcome Margaret.' "[17]

In these lines Miss Jackson sketches the setting for the story, suggests the significance of the house, but never forgets the characters who are a part of that setting. The reader views the scene from the lawn and the bottom of the house up to the tower, the top of the picture. Carla's movement is the framework of the description which ends with the greeting to Margaret and with a continuation of the plot-line of the story.

XII *Use of Irony*

While Miss Jackson's language does not call attention to itself, she depends upon realistic detail to establish an air of authenticity. The setting must be normal, for the characters in it are sometimes *abnormal;* and, characteristically, when both setting and people are realistic (normal), an element of fantasy or a sudden twist may catch the reader off guard. The shock of "The Lottery" is greater because the activities of the villagers seem to be typical of those of small towns everywhere. One of the opening paragraphs describes the following scene:

Soon the men began to gather, surveying their own children, speaking of planting and rain, tractors and taxes. They stood together, away from the pile of stones in the corner, and their jokes were quiet and they smiled rather than laughed. The women, wearing faded house dresses and sweaters, came shortly after their menfolk. They greeted one another and exchanged bits of gossip as they went to join their husbands. Soon the women, standing by their husbands, began to call to their children, and the children came reluctantly, having to be called four or five times.[18]

The activity is not unusual; and, aside from a certain tenseness and an air of excitement, the tone is casual and pleasant. The pleasantness is ironic, considering the seriousness of the matter at hand, but the reader is not aware of the irony until he has read the last paragraphs of the story. The atmosphere remains tense, but sufficiently normal, so that the reader is totally unprepared for the shock of the ending, the stoning of Tessie Hutchinson.

Although Miss Jackson uses various kinds of irony — verbal, dramatic, and situational — throughout her stories, she makes most frequent use of situational irony in which there is the discrepancy between what *is* and what *seems*, or between what one anticipates and what actually comes to pass.

The grandmother stories "Trial by Combat," "Whistler's Grandmother," and "Possibility of Evil" contain situational irony. What the reader expects from the typical little old lady is not what he finds, for these elderly women are deliberately malicious, self-righteously so. Irony is also evident in the incongruities of life and in the duplicities and hypocrisies of ordinary people. In revealing the gap between what is and what seems to be, the author shows her abhorrence of dishonesty, prejudice, and cruelty.

Other stories with a comparable twist are "The Lottery," "On the House," "A Visit," "Charles," "The Bus," "One Ordinary Day with Peanuts," etc. For instance, in the last mentioned story, the reader is surprised to find that Mr. Johnson, having spent the day making people *happy*, is now to reverse roles with his wife, who has just spent her day making people *unhappy*. The stories with the unexpected endings are the most popular and the most anthologized of her works. As with "The Lottery," these seem to be the stories that people remember.

XIII   *Use of Suspense, Mystery, and Ambiguity*

Miss Jackson has gauged her audience's emotional responses and seems to delight in manipulating her readers. For this reason, she appears to be more the entertainer than the conveyor of serious messages. The short stories previously mentioned contain many examples of her use of mystery and ambiguity. For instance, one wonders if the "Daemon Lover" is a phantom or a real man — or is he a product of the protagonist's lively imagination? Any one of these interpretations might be valid, but the reader must decide for himself since no clear-cut answer is given.

In "The Summer People," is the elderly couple, stranded at their summer home after the season, justified in fearing harm from outsiders? There are indications that a plot is set against them; all of the events could be figments of their own imagination, but the reader has no answer. In "The Little House," is the heroine, a new country dweller, justified in fearing that her aunt was murdered and that the murderer may come back for her? Or are these stories simply idle gossip spread by malicious neighbors who hope that she will move back to the city? Are the ghosts in "Home" (the old woman and the boy) intent on harming the Sloanes because they occupy the boy's former home? Are the ghosts real? Naturally, one cannot know.

Each of these stories has been built on suspense, sometimes by withholding information from the reader, at other times by the careful presentation of detail added piece by piece until at the end the picture becomes clear or remains purposely hazy, depending upon the author's intention. For instance, in "The Visit," Miss Jackson gives careful hints throughout that the situation is an unusual one; but, since the reader does not know why, his full realization that Margaret is the only one to have seen the "daytime" ghosts comes as a shock both to him and to Margaret herself. When Margaret asks about the tower, Carla does not answer her questions but continues with other details about the house and Carla's ancestors. "Can we go up to the tower?" Margaret asks, but Carla seems either not to have heard or to be too busy with other information.

As they come to the room with the ceramic-tile floor, Carla points out the picture of a young woman. The inscription beneath it says: "Here was Margaret who died for love." Part One of the story ends on that note. How, the reader wonders, is this picture related to the real Margaret; and the mystery and suspense build. In her wanderings, Margaret visits the tower and meets another Margaret, a great-aunt whose words seem to have double meanings. "He should have come and gone sooner . . . then we'd have it all behind us," she says. Young Margaret, who has just met Carla's brother Paul and his captain friend, assumes the old lady is talking about Paul. Later at a family party, Margaret overhears the old lady and Paul reminiscing about years past. The reader realizes that there is something strange about these two characters, but not until the end of the story does he discover that the captain is Carla's brother and that the other two (Paul and the old lady) are "daylight" ghosts seen only by Margaret. Miss Jackson has spun her tale so skillfully that the incongruities are suspenseful, not incredible to the reader. Suspense and ambiguity are, as one sees, important ingredients also in the full-length works, including the psychological novels.

XIV Symbolism in the Short Stories

It is a mistake to assume that every Jackson story is filled with symbolism. Such stories as "The Visit," "The Rock," and "The Flower Garden" do contain symbolic elements; but many more of her stories do not. And, aside from "The Lottery," which has become a modern classic, the symbolic tales seem to be the least successful. In some instances, the symbols appear too obvious and contrived; in others, objects are emphasized but their significance as symbols is not clear.

In "The Lottery," the symbolism revolves around the ritual of the lottery itself, as an integral part of the whole; and the ritual is the main concern of the story. The little black box, for instance, is the object over which the leader of the tribe mumbles the incantation. The stool beneath the box, which is described as "three-legged," may or may not be significant as a symbol. If so, the stool may be allied to the tripod upon which the sacrifice was placed in the ancient rites for the Egyptian god Re; or possibly it may allude to the Trinity of the Christian Church. Again, if the stool does not carry religious significance (and the reader may take his choice), it may be simply an old-fashioned milking stool, a functional prop of the average farming community, which seems most likely. But the symbolism in "The Lottery" works successfully because it is channeled into the mainstream of the plot, and no extraneous elements call attention to themselves.

Another story, also a fantasy, into whose structure plot and symbolism are closely bound, is "The Rock" (mentioned previously). In this story of three people who journey to an island resort, which turns out to be the home of death, the setting is bleak, the atmosphere, gloomy. In fact, all details of the environment are a signal to the reader that the laws of probability are about to be suspended. Both the island and the lone house on it, the inn, are composed of black rock. Aside from the strange landlady, Death in the person of a Mr. Johnson is the only other visitor at the inn. He is deceptively meek and self-conscious, but he has bold eyes. As in "The Visit," the author has created a separate world, a microcosm, with the characters playing out their roles isolated from the mainland of society. Their journey to the island with the lone boatman is reminiscent of the voyage of mythical characters across the River Styx with Charon to the underground land of Hades. In "The Rock," the network of symbols reinforces the central image of death.

The unification of images is not present, however, in "The Visit"; and the reader is often puzzled as to the significance of certain objects or supposed symbols. For instance, aside from their value to atmosphere, are the various-colored rooms, including the room with the tile floor, representative of anything in particular? Why does Carla's mother embroider the tapestry depicting family members and important family events? Since this story is a fantasy, one cannot examine the details realistically; but the reader is confused by the multiplicity of suggested meanings.

One of the few realistic stories to contain a major symbol is "The Flower Garden." The garden itself parallels the friendship of Mrs. Winning of an old Vermont family and Mrs. MacLane, a young widow who with her young son has just moved from the city. All is well until Mrs. MacLane hires and is friendly with a black man and his son who come daily to take care of the flower garden. Up to this point, and before prejudice enters, the garden has been as beautiful and as productive as the friendship between the two young women; but, as the relationship becomes strained and finally hostile, the garden, too, suffers and is finally destroyed in a storm. Rejected and discouraged, Mrs. MacLane returns to the city. Although the story is valid, the garden symbolism seems contrived and therefore weakens the effect of the whole piece.

Another obvious bit of symbolism is the use of the parrot in "Island" to represent Polly Oakes, Mrs. Montague's nurse-companion; but the parrot is a product of Mrs. Montague's imagination and, therefore, not so objectionable. Otherwise, few of Miss Jackson's stories depend upon symbolism. Of the novels, however, *The Sundial* was criticized for its excessive symbolism, much of which the reviewers were at a loss to explain.

XV *Summary of Characterization*

As has been seen, Miss Jackson views man's nature as basically evil; and she indicates that, in his relationships with his fellow beings, man does not hesitate to lie, cheat, and steal — even to kill when it suits his purposes to do so. As in "The Lottery," he may be persuaded that the evil committed is for the common good; but he nevertheless has the herd instinct and does not oppose the harmful mores of his community. And, sadly enough, man does not improve with age; the grandmothers are as guilty of hyporcrisy and wrongdoing as the younger members of society. In a few stories, young people are the victims, as in "Seven Types of Ambiguity," and "All She Said Was Yes." This situation is reversed in the novels, for in *The Road Through the Wall, The Sundial*, and *We Have Always Lived in the Castle*, adolescents and adults are equally guilty.

One must call Miss Jackson's characters insidious, for they are not openly violent. Their evil is perpetrated or their prejudice exists under the pleasant, smiling guise of an average exterior. They are often quietly dishonest, and the grandmothers are again a good example. Except for fear and contained hatred, these people have no great passions; love and open anger are noticeably absent. Their fears and angry frustrations are not always related to other persons but often to their own needs in adjusting to reality. There is much pettiness in these people, little nobility. Understandably, the majority of protagonists are women. Of these, the career girls are weak, selfish, unlovely. The few men in the stories are the same. The characters who are seemingly strong, wholesome, and confident — such as Mrs. MacLane in "The Flower Garden" and the protagonist of "The Little House" — gradually become the victims of someone else's jealousy, snobbery, or prejudice; and they retreat from the scene.

Miss Jackson does not concern herself with marital problems, but, in the few husband-wife situations, the relationships are strained, as in "The Beautiful Stranger" in which Margaret imagines that a stranger has taken her husband's place. Each individual tends to be isolated in some way; but despite anxieties and loneliness, none of the characters turns to religion and to God for solace. Seemingly, no real God exists in Miss Jackson's fictional universe. Each person is resigned to suffering alone with only dim hope for the future.

Although one can recognize and empathize with the characters in these short stories, one sees them as two-dimensional; few are well-rounded (in contrast with those of the novels). As such, however, they suit the author's purposes, for their functions are often to illustrate a theme or to become part of a suspenseful plot. One remembers few individual persons, but one does remember the stories. In Flannery O'Connor's stories, on the other hand, the reader does not forget Mrs. May in "Greenleaf," the grandmother in "A Good Man Is Hard to Find," or many of the other notable characters. In Miss Jackson's short fiction, the emphasis on theme, rather than on character; an inclination toward the unusual, the mysterious, and the fantastic; a love of suspense and ambiguity; and a need to surprise and shock the reader — all of these elements point toward the storyteller whose primary purpose is to entertain her reader. She is the born teller of tales.

CHAPTER 3

First Novel: The Road Through the Wall

NINETEEN forty-eight, an important year in the Hyman household, was the turning point in the careers of both Shirley Jackson and Stanley Edgar Hyman. Not only was it the year in which Miss Jackson became famous as the author of "The Lottery," but it witnessed also the publication of her first novel, *The Road Through the Wall*. The dedication of this book reads significantly: "For Stanley, a critic"; for in this year Mr. Hyman published *The Armed Vision: A Study in the Methods of Modern Literary Criticism*, a work that quickly established him as an eminent critic.

I *Setting*

The Road Through the Wall is Miss Jackson's only novel to be set in Burlingame, the California town in which she grew up, here called Cabrillo; the year is 1936. The story revolves around the families living on Pepper Street, exposing their private lives, and revealing the often twisted relationships between individuals and among the various households on the block. The climax of the story comes when three-year-old Caroline Desmond is killed and when little Tod Donald, believed responsible for her death, hangs himself. Life will no longer go on as it has, for Pepper Street also is being changed: the wall is being torn down, and the street will now be connected to its counterpart on the other side. Pepper Street, with a wooded area at the back and a high wall to the side, has tended to be fairly well isolated from surrounding areas. As to the inhabitants, "They all lived on Pepper Street because they were able to afford it, and none of them would have lived there if he had been able to afford living elsewhere, although Pepper Street was charming and fairly expensive and even comfortably isolated."

Several of the men daily commute thirty miles to their places of

business in San Francisco; but, to their families and to the other inhabitants, Pepper Street is a microcosm, self-contained, comfortable,
and snug. Through these people, in a minor key, one sees the evils of
mankind. The outwardly pleasant people are not so pleasant, and the
poorer families who periodically rent the one available house next to
the Donalds are always suspect and the objects of prejudice, as are
the Perlmans, the one Jewish family on the block, and young Mrs.
Martin who works somewhere downtown, presumably as a waitress.
Using the omniscient point of view, Miss Jackson presents insight
into the problems and anxieties of the individuals, into the
relationships within families, and into the relative maneuvering of
family groups within the community.

In the prologue, by maplike description, she locates each home
along the street; and this detail lends authenticity to the narrative
and again testifies to Miss Jackson's knowledge of and interest in
houses. The Desmonds, for instance, are the longest-term residents
of the neighborhood and have the largest house:

The Desmond house was on the corner of Pepper Street and Cortez Road,
facing Pepper Street, with a large garden to the side along Pepper Street and
tall blank windows on the Cortez Road side. The tall windows belonged on
the inside to the Desmond livingroom where the family sat in evenings, and
the venetian blinds were always closed after dark. When the Desmonds
moved in, their daughter Caroline had not been born, and the hedge around
the visible sides of the house was inches high. By the time Caroline was
three, the hedge was waist high and required the services of a boy every
Saturday to keep it trimmed. Beyond the hedge the Desmonds lived in a
rambling modern-style house, richly jeweled with glass brick. They were the
aristocracy of the neighborhood, and their house was the largest; their
adopted son Johnny who was fifteen years old, associated with boys whose
families did not live on Pepper Street, but in neighborhoods where the
Desmonds expected to live some day.[1]

This descriptive passage also includes elements of plot; for little
Caroline, introduced casually, becomes the key figure in a tragic
event that destroys not only the complacency but also the composi-
tion of Pepper Street families.

II *Characters: Studies in Cruelty*

The Merriams, who live opposite the Desmonds, are also a proud
family. Fourteen-year-old Harriet Merriam may be the youthful
Shirley Jackson, for she is rather awkward, large, and, as Miss

Jackson thought of herself, unattractive. Harriet writes poetry and stories, and her mother sees that she spends some time writing each day. The fictitious Mrs. Merriam, a righteous, class-conscious, shrewish woman, warns Harriet that she is not to associate with Marilyn Perlman nor is Marilyn ever to come to the house. Marilyn's family, though unforgivably Jewish, is respectable; the family's library is larger than anyone else's on the block; and its home furnishings are equal to those of the Desmonds'. For a time, without Mrs. Merriam's knowledge, Harriet and Marilyn share literary interests and secretly become friends; but, when family pressures end this pleasant relationship, Marilyn is again alone.

The Perlmans are not invited to the lavish garden party given by the Ransome-Joneses for their neighbors, even though the Perlmans live directly across the street. The newest residents of the house for rent, the Terrels, are also ignored. Frederica, the young unattractive girl who seems to take care of all family business, including the actual moving-in; her younger, but larger, mentally retarded sister Beverly, who frequently trudges down the street clutching dollar bills taken from her mother's purse; and a mother whom no one sees, but who apparently spends much time sleeping — these are the members of the Terrel family, people to be laughed at and to become the butt of jokes.

While the adults tend to hide their feelings, the young people are openly cruel. Virginia Donald blatantly mocks Frederica Terrel when they first meet; and Marilyn Perlman, herself long the victim of abuse, recognizes the situation as reversed. She forgets her timidity and turns on Virginia: " 'You shut your fat mouth,' Marilyn said to Virginia. 'You just shut up for once in your life and try to act decent' " (107). Virginia Donald has a tendency to tyrannize over those weaker than she, including her thirteen-year-old brother Tod. Tod, as it turns out, is the figure who precipitates the final tragedy. All his life he has been ignored by others and treated with contempt by his older brother James and his sister:

James Donald privately regarded his younger brother as an imperfect copy of himself, and was as irritated by Tod as he might have been by any cruel, pointed parody. Much of James's athletic sense of good and evil was invested in Tod; Tod was inefficient and a bad sport, which was evil; he was smaller, and could not be struck, which was a delineation of good. . . . Much more, however, of Tod's lack of independent existence was due to his sister Virginia, who was a year older than Tod and his contemporary in a narrower sense than James — she played with the same children, and she hated Tod as

she hated everyone upon whom it was not necessary to intrude her in-
gratiating personality. . . . If Virginia had called Tod names, or refused to
play with him, he would have gained prestige as a participant in a family
fight, but when she seemed to believe sincerely that he had never wholly ex-
isted, he was lost. If he had been able to do any single thing better than
either his brother or his sister, he might have won some small place in the
neighborhood hierarchy, or perhaps even in school. (37 - 38)

Eventually, and ironically, Tod becomes the center of attention in a
manner that, for him, turns into a hideous nightmare.

Many of the older people are also essentially thoughtless and
cruel, some within their own families and others to outsiders. In
several families, the wives dominate their husbands. Mrs. Roberts,
for instance, rails at Mr. Roberts: "She had sat up in bed, late telling
him how he looked to other men, how he disgusted other women,
and had turned, finally, her hair over her eyes and her voice tired,
ready to forgive him, and had found him asleep" (72). Mr. Roberts
has turned to secret affairs with other women, sometimes with their
present maid; and the succession of maids is rapid since Mrs. Roberts
is difficult to please. The latest in the group of maids is a good-
natured high-school girl, Hester Lucas (whether she is meant to
suggest Hester Prynne of the *Scarlet Letter* is uncertain), who has
gained a questionable reputation after running away to be married
and then, two weeks later, being forced home by parental authority.
Hester's family is one of the poorer families whose children must
earn their own living; therefore, she is regarded on Pepper Street as
inferior; and, during her brief stay, she is at the mercy of Mrs.
Roberts.

Like Mrs. Roberts, Mrs. Merriam denigrates her husband, but
with more subtlety. Too righteous and sanctimonious to indulge in
name calling, her treatment of him makes him feel ineffectual and
boorish: " . . . she would look significantly at Harriet when Mr.
Merriam did something indicating his personal coarseness; frequently, often now, Mrs. Merriam would say, 'Never marry a man
who is *inelegant,* Harriet: I can tell you it brings nothing but
sorrow.' If Harriet tried to press her on the subject she would shake
her head and smile sadly; only when she was angry did Mrs.
Merriam permit herself to sink so low as to reproach her husband for
not being daintily bred" (57).

Young Tod Donald's mother thinks of her husband as "helpless,"
and she considers herself clearly superior and the mainstay of the

household. Mr. Donald, having found life full of disappointments, shows little interest in his children; when he wishes to hide, he visits old Mrs. Fielding — two doors down — who also wishes to hide, and they chat for a few quiet moments, sometimes neither listening to the other.

Old Mrs. Fielding is another negative character capable of cruelty. Although outwardly gentle and pleasant, she considers her own interests first and will not upset the routine of her existence to help her neighbors. When Beverly Terrel runs away, and her sister inquires if Mrs. Fielding has seen her, the old lady is panicked; for if she delays her dinner by telling what she knows, the brewing tea will be too strong, the boiled eggs, too hard. So she shuts the door on Frederica.

Miss Tyler, the invalid-sister of Mrs. Ransome-Jones, on the other hand, is deliberately mischievous in seeking a rift between her sister and the man who, she believes, ought to have been hers. Miss Tyler also seriously wounds Harriet Merriam's pride at the garden party by telling her: "You're lucky, you won't ever be pretty. . . . It isn't that you're so *fat*. . . . You just don't have the *air* of a pretty woman. All your life, for instance, you'll walk like you're fat, whether you are or not" (169). Even the next morning, when Harriet awakens to a sense of disaster, the tragedy of Tod and Caroline is not on her mind but the terrible judgment of Miss Tyler.

III *Ambiguity of the Ending*

Miss Jackson is a master of the ambiguous ending, but in this case the ambiguity involves the tragedy — the accident or the crime — that shakes the community and is the climax of events in the novel. During the end of the garden party, Mrs. Desmond is suddenly aware that three-year-old Caroline is missing. Mr. Desmond anxiously visits each house on the block. Characteristically, Mrs. Fielding will not unlock her door and to Mr. Desmond's queries answers only, "I'm sorry . . . I've gone to bed." Meanwhile, Tod Donald, visibly agitated, appears at the Byrne house asking Pat Byrne if he will buy his bicycle for five dollars since he needs money. When Pat refuses, Tod hastily mumbles, "Don't tell anyone," and runs down the street.

Gradually everyone is alerted to the emergency. The police are contacted, and several men organize for the search. Since the danger has not yet been identified, people are aware that their fears may be needless; and, understanding human nature, Miss Jackson describes their ambivalent emotions:

The prevailing mood was one of keen excitement; no one there really wanted Caroline Desmond safe at home, although Mrs. Perlman said crooningly behind Marilyn, 'The poor, poor woman,' and Mrs. Donald said again, 'If we'd only known in time.' Pleasure was in the feeling that the terrors of the night, the jungle, had come close to their safe lighted homes, touched them nearly, and departed, leaving every family safe but one; in acute physical pleasure like a pain, which made them all regard Mr. Desmond greedily, and then turn their eyes away with guilt. (180)

When Tod is suddenly discovered to be missing, Mr. Perlman wonders, "If the two children are together, . . . why didn't the boy bring her home?" But now no one dares pursue the thought aloud until Mr. Desmond asks, "What has he *done* to my little girl?" (182). Not long after this query, Pat Byrne, Mr. Perlman, and two policemen find little Caroline's body among the trees near the creek. Her clothes are splattered with mud; her head is bloody; and there is also blood on the large rock lying next to her.

Tod, hiding behind the brick wall off Cortez Road, wonders if people are looking for him; but the thought seems unlikely to him since no one before had ever made much of a fuss about him and the "principal reason he had not run out and said 'Here I am,' was his fear of the sudden surprise and the humiliating laughter when they saw him and realized that he thought they were looking for him" (184). Later, when the street is empty, he slips across the road, runs home, and hurries to bed. The Donald family, downstairs in the livingroom, hears a noise, investigates, and finds him.

Later the policeman seems to Tod like the doctor, the dentist, and all the persons who have wanted to hurt him. He is petrified and cannot answer the man's questions. Finally, when the policeman says, "Tell me how you killed that little girl. . . . Listen, sonny, we're going to put you in jail," Tod gasps; but the officer then leaves Tod alone in the livingroom to think about the situation until he returns. When almost an hour later the policeman comes back, he finds Tod dead; the boy has taken a piece of the clothesline from the kitchen and has hanged himself. Whether or not the reader finds this action plausible is debatable.

Mrs. Merriam and most of the other Pepper Street inhabitants are sure that Tod had murdered little Caroline. But Pat Byrne wonders if she had perhaps fallen against the rock, had hit her head, and when Tod saw that he couldn't help her he had become frightened. Mr. Perlman thinks the rock too big for Tod to have thrown, and Mr. Merriam remembers that there was no blood on Tod's clothes. He suggests then that it may have been some tramp; but no one knows.

The Donalds and the Desmonds move away. And, as it happens, the tragedy is followed soon after by the finishing of the road that now connects Pepper Street to its counterpart on the other side of the wall. Everyone knows that Pepper Street will never be the same.

IV *Symbolism of the Wall*

The wall, an important feature of the environment, that helps secure the comparative isolation of Pepper Street, is symbolic in several ways. There is something safe about the wall; it offers protection and ensures the social stability of the neighborhood. And, when it becomes clear that outside forces, belonging to the estates enclosed therein, plan to tear down part of the wall, people feel threatened and would stop the project if they could. When the work has begun, the reconstruction is an unsettling influence because of the noise, the presence of the workmen, and the eternal dust that filters over everything. On the other hand, the wall is a dividing line between the moderately prosperous Pepper Street and the great, elegant estates beyond; therefore, those persons with social ambitions and aspirations of wealth dream of moving into the area behind the gates and the wall. The neighborhood there is so exclusive that the streets have no names and the houses no numbers; something like a never-never land, it is also the epitome of material success.

According to Mrs. Mack's Bible, which she reads to her dog, "the wall" is evil; it relates to prejudice and to obstacles man builds to keep him from the grace of God. Mrs. Mack is a strange, sibylic old woman (the children call her a witch); her prophetic readings, spaced at appropriate points in the novel, appear to be commentaries or judgments on the people of the community and on mankind in general. The relationship between Mrs. Mack and her dog is humorous since it parodies the husband-wife situation: she treats the dog like a human, sitting at the table with him, talking to him, scolding him, asking him where he has been, and reading to him. She calls these readings "lessons"; in one instance, she reads: "So will I break down the wall that ye have daubed with untempered mortar, and bring it down to the ground, so that the foundation thereof shall be discovered, and it shall fall and ye shall be consumed in the midst thereof; and ye shall know that I am the Lord. Thus will I accomplish my wrath upon the wall, and upon them that have daubed it with untempered mortar, and will say unto you, 'The wall is no more, neither they that daubed it.' " (121) She then concludes the lesson by asking the dog if he remembers how the Lord destroys evil people. The lesson, presumably, is for all.

A difficulty with the ominiscient viewpoint, when several characters are involved but no specific protagonist, is that the reader receives an overall picture of the situation but never knows any character well enough to become deeply involved in his or her affairs. For example, the reader knows Tod Donald only slightly and Caroline Desmond even less; and the tragedy of their deaths is sad but not so sad as it might have been if one had known them better. Another problem for the reader, because of the various characters and the many families, is the difficulty of keeping the individuals separated. One must check to remember who is who; for instance, besides other children, each of the families — the Robertses, the Donalds, the Merriams, the Martins, and the Williamses — has a fourteen-year-old child important to the story. The Desmonds, besides Caroline, have a fifteen-year-old son. Nonetheless, Miss Jackson's characters are real people, not stereotypes.

Despite the fragmentation of scenes, this novel indicates that Miss Jackson can sustain high reader interest through the longer novel form and that she can create well-rounded characters in a complicated plot. Her task here is rather like that of the juggler, for she manages to keep the many diverse elements of plot and characterization moving and rotating successfully, without dropping or allowing the reader to lose sight of a single one.

Of *The Road Through the Wall*, Robert Halsband said in *The Saturday Review*: " . . . The story is a good one, set down with neither hope nor despair. It is the story of Sidestreet, U.S.A., where the children reflect the life of their parents with its bickering futility and its moral bankruptcy."[2]

CHAPTER 4

The Psychological Novels

I   Hangsaman

BY the time *Hangsaman* was published in 1951, Shirley Jackson was already famous. She had been working on the book some time when she admitted in an interview with *New York Times* correspondent Harvey Breit (June 26, 1949) that she was in the middle of a new novel and was working very slowly at it: "I'm going twice as carefully . . . as I ever did before. I *have* to get it right." That novel was *Hangsaman*, the first of her psychological novels. She had dealt with problems of the mind in short stories, but this novel was her first sustained study of mental aberration, in this case, schizophrenia.

She shows in this novel the disintegration of the mind of Natalie Waite, a brilliant, seventeen-year-old girl. Natalie's father Arnold, a writer-critic, is the dominating influence in her life, and it is he who chooses the liberal girls' college, rather like Bennington, at which she can be *educated to live*, a process whereby the adolescent learns to adjust to the adult world. From the beginning, Natalie is an outsider; she wants desperately to make friends, but, because of her superior intellect and her shy nature, she is different from most of the girls at school. She finds a hero/father substitute in her literature teacher, Arthur Langdon; but she is soon disillusioned about him when she discovers that her idol treats his wife badly. Alone and unhappy, she confesses her real feelings in her diary and then finds or creates a friend, Tony, with whom she can talk and feel comfortable. She and Tony decide to leave the college to go off somewhere by train, but instead, they take a bus to the outskirts of town, a lonely wooded area. Here Natalie becomes terrified during a confrontation with Tony and flees from the scene. Getting a ride back to town and then walking back to the college, she begins to feel hope and reassurance. She has, supposedly, gained some insight into her problems.

Miss Jackson's love of mystery and ambiguity is evident in this novel, for the reader receives only piecemeal information as Natalie sees it. There are gaps, therefore, in his knowledge. Suspense builds, and the mystery deepens with the appearance of Tony; but, even by the end of the novel, there is confusion as to who Tony is and as to what has actually taken place. Only at the end of the narrative does the reader discover that Tony is and has been a product of Natalie's imagination or, technically, another aspect of Natalie's self.

Miss Jackson cleverly conceals this fact from the reader, for Natalie speaks of Tony as if she were a real girl. To her father, she writes: "There is a very strange character around here who would interest you very much. She is always off by herself somewhere, and when I asked someone about her they laughed and said, 'Oh, that's that girl Tony Something.' I keep seeing her around and I think I would like to meet her."[1] Later in the same letter she says again: "Speaking of magic, I figure that now I have once mentioned that I would like to meet that girl Tony, I will certainly meet her soon. I have discovered that all you have to do is notice a thing like that concretely enough to say it, as in a letter like this, for it to happen. I suppose once I meet her I will be disappointed" (121).

Natalie, one discovers, is superstitious but also aware that the mind may have strange powers. Nevertheless, that night in unusual circumstances she meets Tony. She says to her father: "By the way, you remember Tony? The girl I wrote you about? Well, I finally met her and I like her a lot. She lives in a house on the other side of the campus and yesterday afternoon we walked about four miles through country just beyond the campus. I think she's terribly interesting" (131).

Tony appears again to Natalie one night as Natalie sits outside on the front steps of the Langdon house while a party is going on inside. When Natalie asks Tony if she were invited to the party, Tony says no and soon leaves. As Natalie goes back to the festivities, Elizabeth Langdon, who has come to look for her, says: "I saw you with someone." This statement (in hindsight) is confusing, since it seems to prove that there is an actual Tony — unless Elizabeth only assumes that she saw someone in the darkness. But the reader, at this point, does not question the existence of Tony, mysterious though she may be.

Again, the evening before their trip to the railroad station, Natalie visits Tony, who, one is told, is sitting cross-legged on the bed playing solitaire with the Tarot cards. Natalie, who has just returned

from a disappointing visit at home over the Thanksgiving holidays,
says to Tony:

> "I'm sorry, I really am. I came to say I was terribly, terribly sorry. I
> shouldn't have gone, and I'm sorry."
> "I'm never *really* angry with you anyway," Tony said.
> "Of course."
> "I told you they would be. Did they hang on you?"
> "They were all there. Even my brother. They fed me," Natalie said.
> "They didn't do anything else except feed me, I think." (156)

This conversation, purposely sketchy, requires the reader to supply
details from his own imagination; but, as before, the narration of the
whole scene is misleading. Miss Jackson almost compels her
audience to believe in a *real* Tony when she writes that "Tony and
Natalie believed that they were the only two people in the world
who now loved Tarot cards and used them — so reminiscent of an-
tique, undreamed games — for games of their own, invented card
games, and walking games, and a kind of affectionate fortune-telling
which was always faithful to the meanings of the cards as recorded in
the Tarot book, but which somehow always came out as meaning
that Tony and Natalie were the finest and luckiest persons im-
aginable" (156). The longer, more complicated sentences used in the
impressionistic portions of the novel tend to reinforce the mystery
and ambiguity. At any rate, Tony then, apparently, reads Natalie to
sleep: "Much, much later, Natalie was sound asleep aware of Tony's
slipping into the bed beside her. Side by side, like two big cats, they
slept."

The previous passage seems to confirm the reality of two separate
girls. The adventures in the railroad station follow and then the bus
ride into the countryside to the ultimate confrontation between the
"two" girls. Natalie says:

> "Where in the hell are we?" . . . she was cross and it was colder than she
> liked, and she was unpleasantly aware that that had probably been the last
> bus back to town.
> "Look," said Tony . . . "if you don't want to come you don't have to. I'm
> going anyway." (181)

After Natalie follows Tony into a dark, wooded area, she seems to
lose sight of her. When the figure she thought was Tony is only
another tree, she is frightened. She calls again, but there is no

answer. She stumbles on, coming then into a clearing. Again she sees Tony: "Without stumbling as though permitted, Tony came walking easily through the trees and not by the path, seeming not to put her feet down on the soundless moss." (186) In these passages, the reader begins to sense a strangeness about Tony; she no longer seems human.

Natalie suddenly feels that Tony is the agent of some black secret force, a traitor, and that she has been commissioned to bring Natalie here. When Natalie is afraid and wants to go back, " 'Later,' Tony said peacefully, the unrepentent traitor, the traitor of traitors. 'Later I might let you go back' " (188). When Natalie wonders if she is to be sacrificed and remarks that "I thought it was a game," Tony tells her to "keep thinking of it as a game," and says that she can leave if she is afraid. Later, when Natalie calls to Tony again and receives no answer, Natalie turns back along the path. She has, she believes, seen the last of Tony: " 'I will never see Tony any more; she is gone,' and knew that theatrical or not, it was true. She had defeated her own enemy, she thought, and she would never be required to fight again, and she put her feet down tiredly in the mud and thought, What did I do wrong?" (188).

The sole clue to the character of Tony is in this scene in the woods. Natalie's terror brings the realization that she must flee from Tony, who is now elusive and unreal, appearing and disappearing, walking without seeming to put her feet down. As she leaves, she feels that she has triumphed in some way, that she has defeated her enemy. She will never see Tony again. If Tony were real, of course, she would eventually come back to the campus. But, because of the ambiguity and mystery throughout the novel, critics have been confused as to the character of Tony, and they have given varying interpretations to the story. In his book *The College Novel in America* (1962), John O. Lyons assumes not only that Tony is a flesh-and-blood figure but that she is a Lesbian; and he interprets this last scene in the woods as an attempted seduction.[2] The objection to this view is that Natalie and Tony need not have come to the woods for an affair since they could have remained safe and warm in their own dormitory room; nor does an affair explain the mysterious appearances and disappearances of Tony, nor take into account the steadily deteriorating state of Natalie's mind. What then would be the point to the novel? That Natalie's adventures simply represent an initiation into life is not a satisfactory interpretation. The freshman initiation ceremony is a brief but disturbing event for

Natalie since she considers the proceedings ridiculous and walks out on them. Her other experiences fail as initiations into reality also, for her reactions and behavior are not those of a normal, healthy teenager.

Alice S. Morris in her *New York Times* review "Adventure Into Reality" (April 22, 1951) assumes also that Tony is an actual girl. Miss Morris praises the author's masterful writing, her true-to-life characters, calling the novel a work of "artistic maturity." There is, she claims, no false note; however, she does not attempt to either explain or deal with the scene in the woods.³ Most reviewers, such as Florence Haxton Bullock (*New York Herald Tribune Book Review*) and the staff writer of *Time* magazine, assumed that Tony was an aspect of Natalie's madness. W. T. Scott *(Saturday Review)* indicated more clearly than anyone else the root of the novel's problem when he observed that Natalie obviously has schizoid tendencies (as note her diary) but that it is difficult to be certain whether Tony is real or imagined since Miss Jackson has not fully prepared the reader for the jump from Natalie's lucid, though disturbed behavior to the later vague and seemingly complete madness.⁴

Miss Jackson seems to have withheld information deliberately for the purposes of suspense and a shock-value ending. Up to a point, there are definite clues as to Natalie's affliction since she exhibits strange behavior in a number of ways. Since the age of fifteen, one learns, she has created private worlds of her own: "Natalie Waite . . . lived in an odd corner of a world of sound and sight past the daily voices of her father and mother and their incomprehensible actions. For the past two years . . . she had lived completely by herself, allowing not even her father access to the farther places of her mind. She visited strange countries, and the voices of their inhabitants were constantly in her ear; when her father spoke he was accompanied by strange laughter, unheard probably by anyone except his daughter" (6). When she is confronted by ideas that are not particularly appealing, such as being married with children of her own, she drives away the ugly thoughts: "She brought herself away from the disagreeably clinging thought by her usual method — imagining the sweet sharp sensation of being burned alive . . ."(11).

Natalie is undeniably hostile in many ways. One sees this again at the regular Sunday afternoon cocktail party given by her parents, when she converses with her father and the guests and, at the same time, playfully carries on a mental dialogue with a detective, imagining herself involved in a murder case in which she is the murderer. Several weeks later, as she is crossing the campus at night, she imagines that she has created a world of little manikins of the people she knows, and they are now at her mercy. She imagines herself tearing their houses apart, pulling off arms and legs, chewing on the "small sweet bones." She, herself, has been a victim of a seduction in the early evening of one of the cocktail parties at home when she willingly wandered off with one of the guests; but, because her thoughts are fragmented, one never knows the exact circumstances. Miss Jackson moves on then to the next morning when Natalie vows that she will not remember what has happened; and, since no more attention is given the incident, one cannot gauge the impact of the trauma or its long-lasting effects.

Natalie's relationships with her family are unusual. She is fond of her dominating father but recognizes perhaps, that he can be ridiculous; she is distantly friendly and often uncomfortable with her younger brother Bud; she does not like to be alone with her mother. At breakfast, for instance, after her father and brother have left the table, leaving Natalie with her mother, her reaction assures the reader that she is somewhat strange: "Terror lest she be left alone with her mother made Natalie almost speechless; as her mother opened her mouth to speak (perhaps to say, 'Excuse me,' to Natalie; perhaps she was as much troubled by being left alone with Natalie) Natalie said quickly, 'Busy now,' and went with little dignity out of the French doors behind her chair and down the flat steps into the garden" (9). At this point, Natalie has nothing to hide; her mother, though often alcoholic, has nothing but kind words for her daughter. The only reasonable explanation for Natalie's violent emotions seems to be that she is displaying symptoms of the mental disorder that becomes a severe one within a short time.

Her college experiences increase her nervousness and her sense of aloneness. Her lack of friends is not due solely to her outward self-assurance and intellectual superiority, for she seeks no one and withdraws more and more into the recesses of her creative imagination. The reader is not fully aware of Natalie's discontentment, for she seems willing to spend her time writing regular letters to her father, jotting entries in her journal, and studying. It is something of a shock then to learn — through Rosalind — what the other girls in the house think of Natalie:

"Well, you know what they say about *you*. . . . They say you're crazy. You sit here in your room all day and all night and never go out and they say you're crazy."

"I go out to class," Natalie said quickly.

"They say you're spooky," Rosalind said. "That's what they call you, Spooky, I heard them!" (61)

Without rejecting Rosalind, Natalie says that all she wants is to be left alone and that what the others think is not at all important. However, this statement appears to be a rationalization; for she thinks otherwise:

Even as she spoke she knew her position, and her mind, racing ahead of her, was counting over its special private blessings: there was her father, of course, although he seemed, right now, far away and helpless against laughing girls, there was Arthur Langdon and the fact that she seemed, more than any other, to be comprehending and alert in his class, and had received a sort of recognition, as though they were kindred, from him — but then perhaps, she thought, frightened, perhaps not everyone thought of Arthur Langdon's regard as special. Perhaps he was not so valuable to these watching, laughing girls as other things Natalie had never heard of. But then, of course, there was always and beyond all laughter and beyond all scrutiny her own sweet dear home of a mind, where she was safe, protected, priceless. . . . "They're trivial people, really. Mediocre." (62)

Aggravated symptoms of mental stress and schizoid tendencies appear in Natalie's secret journal when the inner Natalie addresses her outer self, as if they were separate individuals:

Dearest dearest darling most important dearest darling Natalie — this is me talking, your own priceless own Natalie, and I just wanted to tell you one single small thing: you *are* the best, and they *will* know it someday, and someday no one will ever dare laugh again when you are near, and no one will dare even *speak* to you without bowing first. And they will be afraid of you. And all you have to do is wait, my darling, wait and it will come, I promise you. Because that's the fair part of it — they have it now, and you have it later. Don't worry, please, please don't, because worrying might spoil it, because if you worry it might not come true. (64)

As the journal continues, the writer tells Natalie not to despair; but then no more is written about her troubled thoughts since the next scenes shift to her philosophy and music classes. Thirty pages pass before one finds further mention of Natalie's secret self in another journal entry. In the meantime, outwardly, she functions well. She meets and becomes friends with the unhappy Elizabeth Langdon, the wife of her literature professor.

In a mid-October journal entry, Natalie records that she is no longer afraid and dares to be alone. At the same time, she tells her father about Tony. As far as the reader can judge, outwardly, all goes smoothly during the Thanksgiving holidays at home; but Natalie seems restless and leaves earlier than she had originally planned. She later admits to her father that she is doing poorly at school, but she does not admit her true thoughts — that she is a failure and hates college and everyone around her. At this point, Miss Jackson provides some hitherto unknown information about the extent of Natalie's estrangement from the other girls. For instance, when Natalie gets back to the dormitory, she hides under the stairs to avoid the girls as they go to dinner. At some time past, she has apparently been humiliated at dinner by girls who did not wish to sit with her; and she has not gone to the dining hall since then. Also, now one learns that Natalie has rearranged her room; impatient with the lack of space, she has packed her clothes in the suitcase in the closet. She has pushed the dresser, the armchair, and the bookcase into the hall to be taken away. She has moved her bed under the window and has crammed the desk and chair into a corner. She has, furthermore, hung her wastebasket outside her window but has tied it by a string to the head of her bed. Moreover, she keeps her door locked; and she has not been to class in two weeks. At this juncture, she supposedly visits Tony and then goes away the following day to the railroad station and to the countryside. These circumstances, which show Natalie in a different light, indicate the seriousness of her problems. Even though Natalie's affliction has progressed steadily, the reader has not known until almost the end the extent of her illness. For this reason, and because Tony has been treated as a real, though mysterious, girl, the realization that Natalie is schizoid comes as a shock.

A question arises also as to the conclusion of the novel, for the ending seems not only too expedient but not altogether plausible. Natalie, after the scene in the woods, has received a ride to town as far as the bridge. Fascinated by the dark waters below, she tries to climb the wall but is dissuaded when she sees people approaching. "Going swimming?" someone asks. This reaction is the only indication that Natalie may be considering suicide, but one does not know how seriously she has been shocked by the confrontation with Tony. She continues toward the school, and finally she can see the college buildings: "The reassuring bulk of the college buildings showed ahead of her, and she looked fondly up at them and smiled. As she had never been before, she was now alone, and grown-up, and powerful, and not at all afraid" (191). On this note the story ends, seemingly hopeful, with Natalie shocked into an awareness of herself and of what has happened to her. If hers is a temporary optimism and a temporary recovery, how long can her state last? Is almost instant recovery plausible? The reader can only wonder. There is, however, a definite change in tone from the comparative realism of the first portions of the novel to the mental fantasizing in the latter parts.

As in *The Road Through the Wall*, this novel contains rapid, fragmented changes of scene with the difference that here the viewpoint is third person, but the point of view is limited to Natalie. In both works, the reader receives bits and pieces of information; but, in *Hangsaman*, as in some of the short stories, it is difficult to separate the several planes of reality.

Despite minor objections, the critics were impressed with the book. Paul Pickrel in the *Yale Review* called *Hangsaman* an outstanding novel, an "extraordinary, perceptive picture of adolescence," but one must point out that Mr. Pickrel concentrated on the first portion of the book and ignored the problems of the second half. On the other hand, he may not have considered the areas in question to be serious problems.[5]

The title of the book may have been suggested by the hanging man of the Tarot cards, a favorite game of Natalie-Tony. They see, also, in a toy shop window a figure that turns and swings "around and around, endlessly and irritatingly." The little figure may well be symbolic of Natalie's own mental convolutions and the condition of being trapped. The actual term "Hangsaman," however, is used in an old English ballad, one stanza of which is printed opposite the title page:

> Slack your rope, Hangsaman,
> O slack it for a while,
> I think I see my true love coming,
> Coming many a mile.

In one version of this ballad, "father" is substituted for "true love"; and perhaps that word might have been more appropriate in this case. The use of portions of ballads and ballad refrains to underline major ideas is a frequent practice in Shirley Jackson's work, especially in the novels. One of the refrains that recurs significantly throughout *Hangsaman* is the line "One is one and all alone and evermore shall be so." This truth is the one that Natalie must eventually accept.

II   The Bird's Nest

Three years after *Hangsaman*, critics applauded the appearance in 1954 of Miss Jackson's second psychological novel, *The Bird's Nest*, although certain reviewers believed the earlier book to be superior. As she had with *Hangsaman*, Miss Jackson spent many hours studying dissociation: schizophrenia and the multiple personality. In a letter (1954) to her mother, she stated: "I did a good deal of background reading before I wrote the book and one area of hysterical behavior I know backward and forward is the dissociated personality." The Bennington College psychologist had supplied her with books and advice, and the actual case history that became the basis for the study of Elizabeth-Beth-Betsy-Bess was a 1906 study by Dr. Morton Prince entitled *The Dissociation of a Personality*. As Miss Jackson's fictitious Dr. Wright says in his journal (quoting from the actual study of Dr. Prince),

Cases of this kind are commonly known as "double" or "multiple personality," according to the number of persons represented, but a more correct term is *disintegrated* personality, for each secondary personality is a part only of a normal whole self. No one secondary personality preserves the whole physical life of the individual. The synthesis of the original consciousness known as the personal ego is broken up, so to speak, and shorn of some of its memories, perceptions, acquisitions, or modes of reaction to the environment. The conscious states that still persist, synthesized among themselves, form a new personality capable of independent activity. This second personality may alternate with the original undisintegrated personality from time to time. By a breaking up of the original personality at different moments along different lines of cleavage, there may be formed several different secondary personalities which may take turns with one another.[6]

As in *Hangsaman*, the title of the book comes from a verse, this time an old riddle that reads:

> Elizabeth, Lizzy, Betsy and Bess
> All went together to see a bird's nest;
> They found a nest with five eggs in it;
> They each took one and left four in it.

The answer, of course, is that the four names apply to the one girl, whose personalities, in this instance, are almost separate and complete.

The novel is divided into six sections, each of which is named after and assimilates the point of view of the principal character of that section. In the first part, "Elizabeth," Miss Jackson uses limited, omniscient point of view — that of Elizabeth; but Miss Jackson feels free to make general comments about the surroundings and the situation in which the twenty-three-year-old girl finds herself. Drab and colorless, Elizabeth Richmond works on the third sagging floor of a museum that is undergoing emergency reconstruction. Subject to severe headaches and backaches, she has not been well since her mother died four years before and left her (though in comfort) alone with her mother's sister, Aunt Morgen, in whose home she and her mother had lived since her father's death, when Elizabeth was two years old.

Throughout this novel there are touches of the Jackson humor, not only in the author's comments but in the characters of Aunt Morgen and Dr. Wright, the psychiatrist in the case. For instance, Miss Jackson broaches Elizabeth's problem in the following manner: "It is not proven that Elizabeth's personal equilibrium was set off balance by the slant of the office floor, nor could it be proven that it was Elizabeth who pushed the building off its foundations, but it is undeniable that they began to slip at about the same time" (150). In addition to the physical ailments, Elizabeth is suddenly plagued with nasty scrawled notes left on her desk at the office, such as: "dear lizzie . . . your fools paradise is gone now for good watch out for me lizzie watch out for me and dont do anything bad because i am going to catch you and you will be sorry and dont think i wont know lizzie because i do — dirty thoughts lizzie dirty lizzie" (151).

Elizabeth collects these letters and keeps them with a seven-year-old letter of her mother's in a red cardboard valentine box on the shelf of her closet. Aunt Morgen, in the meantime, becomes increasingly concerned as Elizabeth pretends innocence and denies sneaking out of the house in the middle of the night. And when quiet ladylike Elizabeth, after a few sherrys, which she normally does not drink, loudly insults their hosts for the evening, Aunt Morgen insists that Elizabeth visit a doctor. Their family physician suggests Dr. Wright.

In the second section, entitled "Doctor Wright," the point of view changes to first person and is presented as part of the doctor's case study. This angle of narration permits him (and Miss Jackson) to inject opinion and to expose the reader to Dr. Wright's warmhearted humor. In certain respects, Dr. Wright resembles Mr. Waite, Natalie's father in *Hangsaman:* both men are verbal, erudite, and pompous; but the doctor takes himself less seriously and is, therefore, a more likable person. He writes of himself:

I make no excuses or apologies for my medical views, although perhaps my literary style will leave something to be desired, and I preface this account by saying, as I have said for forty years or more, that an honest doctor is an honest man, and considers his patient's welfare before the bills are sent in. My own practice has dwindled because most of my patients are dead — (that is another of my little jokes, and we'll have to get used to them, reader, before you and I can go on together; I am a whimsical man and must have my smile) — naturally, because they grew old along with me, and I survived 'em, being a medical man. (176)

The doctor's literary style, as one critic rightly points out, is something of a parody of Thackeray's, Dr. Wright's favorite author.

Using his special "hobbyhorse," hypnosis, as a means of interviewing, Dr. Wright gradually determines that Elizabeth has three distinct personalities — and still later he discovers a fourth one, which is more disagreeable than any of the others — Bess. The first personality is the dull, ladylike, subdued Elizabeth; the second, and Dr. Wright's favorite, is Beth, a cheerful, attractive, intelligent girl; the third is Betsy, roguish, often rude, full of pranks, sly and not particularly cooperative; the last is Bess, cold, calculating, ruthless, entirely occupied with thoughts of money and the fortune she is to inherit at twenty-five.

As the sessions progress, Betsy, particularly evil, coarse, and sensuous, seems the strongest personality; but each of the fragmented selves struggles to be recognized and to make itself known. Dr. Wright dreads Betsy who, one finds, has been responsible for Elizabeth's aches and pains and the poison-pen notes. The severe emotional shock, the factor responsible for the disintegration of the original Elizabeth, seems to have been the death of her mother. Betsy, however, does not accept the fact that her mother is dead; and, at the end of section two, she tricks Dr. Wright and Aunt Morgen by pretending to be ill; then, with packed suitcase, she hurries off in the night to take a bus to New York.

Section three, "Betsy" (written in third person as seen through Betsy's eyes), is devoted to the New York experience. Established in the comfortable hotel Aunt Morgen uses during her New York trips, Betsy has one purpose — to find her mother. She tries vainly to remember details of the days when she, a two-year-old, lived there with her mother. In a stream-of-consciousness flow, she wanders off in search of the house — with a pink room — overlooking the river. She asks directions from people in the street and inquires at specific houses chosen from arbitrary information and surmise. During the search, she is aware that great blocks of time have passed for which she cannot account. Although the reader receives the background information slowly and by piecemeal, he begins to understand the nature of Elizabeth's problem.

Mother Elizabeth has had a boyfriend, Robin, who was not particularly fond of the young Elizabeth; to him, she was in the way and a "nuisance." As Elizabeth grew older, she thought of herself as a rival for Robin's affections; but she had, unless the incident is purely imagined, an affair with Robin before she supposedly chased him away by threatening to tell her mother. Now, running through the streets, she constantly identifies herself with her mother. Twice she flees in terror, imagining that she sees Robin coming toward her. Sometimes she thinks of Robin fondly, wanting him to call her by her mother's nickname. Finding her way back to the hotel, she is aware that her room is in a shambles: her clothes are ripped and scattered about; the curtains have been torn down; the sheets are in shreds; the pillows are leaking feathers. She realizes that someone within her body is trying desperately to gain the upper hand with the intention perhaps of going back home.

As a result, Betsy and the unknown "she" struggle for the key of the room (the door is locked); and Betsy is badly scratched, bruised, and choked. These are self-inflicted wounds, Dr. Wright — some time later — realizes; but now, after passing out, Elizabeth awakens to find herself in a hospital where the nurses and doctors assume that she has been the victim of a criminal attack. A slip of paper in Elizabeth's pocket with Dr. Wright's name and address prompts the staff to call him. The "she" who has struggled with Betsy, however, is the newest of the personalities and the one with whom Dr. Wright has not yet come in contact. "Who in sin are you?" she asks as he comes into her room. These words, baffling to the doctor, end the section on Betsy and renew, as Miss Jackson does so expertly, the suspense.

In section four, "Dr. Wright," which resumes the first-person-case-history technique used in part two, Bess, the new self, becomes

a serious problem. She is at present the strongest and the most ob-
noxious of the four; she is hostile to both Aunt Morgen and Dr.
Wright; and she is the arch enemy of Betsy and determined to
emerge as the dominant personality. Bess is symbolic of the forces of
evil, and the formerly satanic Betsy now becomes allied to the forces
of good; as the struggle between them increases, the suspense also
mounts. Betsy plays practical jokes on Bess, hoping to discredit her
with Aunt Morgen and with Dr. Wright who already deplores the
possibility that Bess may become the permanent Elizabeth.
Although the reader is not always conscious of the time span involving the treatment of Elizabeth, he receives a clue now and then
from the doctor's notes. Twenty months have apparently passed
since Elizabeth's first visit, and it will be twenty-eight or twenty-
nine months before the successful integration of the selves.

One of the highlights of this portion of the book is the visit Dr.
Wright feels obligated to pay to Aunt Morgen Jones to talk over
Elizabeth's case. Heretofore there has been little direct communica-
tion between them, for Dr. Wright has avoided her as long as he
could. Morgen is a warmhearted woman with a mind of her own.
Earlier in the novel, Miss Jackson describes her in the following way:

Although Aunt Morgen was the type of woman freely described as
"masculine," if she had been a man she would have cut a very poor figure
indeed. If she had been a man she would have been middle-sized, weak-
jawed, shifty-eyed, and clumsy; fortunately, having been born not a man,
she had turned out a woman, and had of necessity adopted from adolescence
(with what grief, perhaps, and frantic railings against the iniquities of fate,
which made her sister lovely) the personality of the gruff, loud-voiced
woman so invariably described as "masculine." Her manner was free, her
voice loud, she loved eating and drinking and said she loved men; she took
toward her sober niece an attitude of avuncular heartiness, and among her
few friends she was regarded as fairly dashing because of her fondness for
blunt truths and her comprehensive statements about baseball. (155)

Dr. Wright, the widower, is also opinionated; he has previously
thought of Morgen Jones as "a singularly unattractive woman,
heavy-set and overbearing with a loud laugh and a gaudy taste in
clothes." He considers her house an abomination; as he says in his
journal: "I do not mean to say merely that Miss Jones' home was
ugly; to my mind it was hideous." He objects especially to a life-size
"unclad" figure in black wood in the front hall with an unlovely
physique that he suspects might well have been a representation of

Miss Jones herself except that the statue's head has no hair (later, as he comes to know her better, he persuades her to put the figure in the attic). The conference begins in friendly but serious fashion while she serves brandy in goblet glasses.

Several goblets later, their attitude toward each other has mellowed as they still discuss the various Elizabeths and Morgen's sister, Elizabeth's mother. Both women apparently had been in love with Elizabeth's father, who has put his money in trust in Morgen's care for his daughter; the estate is to be Elizabeth's when she is twenty-five, a matter now of two more months. Mother Elizabeth, one discovers, was a woman who drank heartily, had many affairs, and was often absent from the household. On the morning of the day she died, her birthday, she had been absent for two nights and a day; and she had appeared at the door only to be met by an angry Elizabeth who had furiously shaken her mother. The shaking, Morgen says, did not harm her; nevertheless, Morgen managed to maneuver the young girl into her bedroom and to lock the door. Mother Elizabeth, they found, was seriously ill and died that afternoon. Of the "girls," Betsy has not yet accepted her mother's death; and Bess believes that the six-year-old event occurred only "three weeks ago."

Section five, entitled "Aunt Morgen," centers on the activities and the conflicts at home; for Aunt Morgen is doing her best to remain cheerful despite the growing tension and the open warfare between Bess and Betsy. When Aunt Morgen opens the refrigerator to find it full of mud, or when she discovers she has a mud-filled sandwich, she simply absorbs a few more brandies and goes to bed. In some instances, Betsy is the culprit, but one never really knows why she chose pranks to irritate Aunt Morgen; for she, Aunt Morgen, Elizabeth, and Beth are aligned against Bess, who is getting stronger and meaner every day. Immune to a kind gesture, as when her aunt says she can have money to go out to dinner anywhere she likes, Bess replies: " 'You don't know how I'm going to get even with you someday.' . . . She spoke slowly, and she looked at her aunt with hatred. 'You don't know all the things I've been thinking of to do to you. When I have all my money, and I don't have to live with you any more, I'm going to spend half my time doing nasty things to you' " (329).

Morgen is not easily threatened; and soon after, when she proposes a good spanking, Bess retires, making way for the quiet Elizabeth. Morgen manages to retain her sense of humor: in a particularly funny scene, she runs the bath water as each of the Elizabeths, one after the other, takes a separate bath, each borrowing Morgen's bath salts (the separate personalities are not always conscious of what the others are doing).

The novel reaches a climax when Morgen realizes that she can no longer cope with the situation but must send Elizabeth to an institution and, therefore, calls Dr. Wright for help. A confrontation with Bess and Betsy ensues in which Aunt Morgen forces them to talk about their mother's death; this scene is followed by the vicious attempt of Betsy to scratch Bess's eyes out; and, after a violent struggle in which both Dr. Wright and Aunt Morgen hold and subdue the girl, they seem to be left with the personality of Elizabeth. On that uncertain note, this portion of the book ends.

The last — rather anticlimactic — section, "The Naming of An Heiress," takes place three months later and is devoted to the eventual integration of the new personality. She is suddenly conscious of being alone (Miss Jackson refers to her now as "she"). She thinks: "I am — and it was her first privately phrased thought — all alone; it was clear and sparkling as cold water, and she said it again to herself: I am all alone" (359). Apparently, the state of feeling alone is synonymous with health, just as it is with Natalie in *Hangsaman* when she rids herself of the influence of Tony. As the new "she" gains confidence, she follows the impulse to cut her long hair; and seems to shed with this symbolic gesture the unhappy connection with the past. "I know who I am," she says.

In this novel, as in previous works, the fragmentation of scenes and personalities persists. The multiple-character point of view is largely responsible for the shifting emphasis, but it also contributes to the depth of the novel. The flashbacks are cleverly integrated, often with present action as in Betsy's New York trip. While she rushes about in search of her mother, she remembers portions of her childhood experiences, but she often invents what she wishes to believe. The reader gradually puts the pieces in place and, by the end, "seems" to know what has happened. As in the other novels, Miss Jackson has withheld vital information until the end, thereby maintaining suspense and ensuring the ambiguous quality of the work. Nonetheless, each character is unique and believable, a major achievement considering the difficulties in presenting the four persons of Elizabeth's disintegrated self. Dr. Wright and Aunt Morgen supply much humor in their lovable yet competing personalities. Both are headstrong characters with obvious, but human, flaws.

102 SHIRLEY JACKSON

In a review in the *New York Herald Tribune* (June 20, 1954), Dan Wickendan indicates his appreciation of Miss Jackson's humor, noting that she writes novels that are unique in that the drama is often underlined by humor and the comedy is often one with pathos. He calls the climax of *The Bird's Nest* and its conclusion "curiously moving." The book as a whole he calls "superlative entertainment," much the best book that she has written.[7] Several other critics agreed that this novel is a better one than either *The Road Through the Wall* or *Hangsaman.* It is indicative of Miss Jackson's storytelling abilities that she could produce a sound psychological case history that is also excellent entertainment.

But perhaps the most enlightening and sensitive analysis of the book is that by William Peden in *The Saturday Review* (July 17, 1954);

Miss Jackson has done much more than produce just another perceptive clinical study of emotional deterioration. She has created a kind of twentieth-century morality play in which the familiar medieval conflict between good and evil has been replaced by the struggle for domination among Elizabeth, Beth, Betsy and Bess. This struggle is illuminated throughout by a remarkable sense of humor (witness the crackling high comedy of the drinking scene between Morgen Jones and Dr. Wright) which places the author closer in spirit to Jane Austen than one might at first think possible (a cynical Jane Austen to be sure, more familiar with Freud than with Fanny Burney, and more concerned with evil than with tea table courtships). And like Jane Austen, Miss Jackson no longer creates primarily to analyze and dissect. Her novel suggests that without the love and understanding that eventually restore Elizabeth, existence can become a disorderly bird's nest of fears, doubts, and wrong moves as meaningless and confusing as the 17th-century riddle from which "The Bird's Nest" derives its title.[8]

The new Elizabeth does have security and people who love and understand her. Also, she is more fortunate than Natalie in that she need not compete with others. Although the passage of time is not emphasized in the book, the process of therapy and integration covers a period of two-and-a-half years, making her recovery more plausible than Natalie's partial recovery of self in *Hangsaman.* Yet, reviewer Edmund Fuller, while praising the book, was not fully convinced as to the probability of the ending (*Chicago Sunday Tribune*, June 27, 1954): " . . . Her portrayal of a personality in disintegration is masterful. I am not wholly sold on the simplicity of its resolution, but this is a minor reservation in the face of a considerable achievement."[9]

The news that Metro-Goldwyn-Mayer had purchased the book for a film production caused a mild stir in the Hyman household, and Shirley Jackson in her characteristic manner concentrated on the humorous aspects in relating the details in a letter to her mother:

It says in the contract that I have nothing whatsoever to say about any aspect of the movie, and do not even get free passes. I do not plan to see it, myself, but my agent proposes that they have the grand premiere at the General Stark Theatre in Bennington, if they can get the bats out of the lobby. Everyone around here was very excited for about a day, and then of course lost interest when it turned out that there was no amazing amount of money involved and no one was going to have to fly to Hollywood and no movie stars were going to be hanging around upper Main Street in North Bennington. . . . I have read the screen play and it sounds a little like Ma and Pa Kettle or Abbot and Costello meet a multiple personality. The college psychologist, who lent me books and gave me much good advice for the book, says he is going to shoot himself.[10]

Later, after seeing the movie, *Lizzie*, she complains ruefully:

Practically the only lines of mine they left in are the ones for Joan Blondell, who is the old aunt; she sits there with a fifth of bourbon and babbles. They must have used up twenty cases of bourbon in the movie; there are shots of people carrying out bushel baskets of empty bottles. Stanley says it is because in Hollywood they don't know anything about drinking because they all take dope. They don't know much about psychology either.[11]

CHAPTER 5

Novels of Setting:
The House as a Personality

WELL-BUILT old houses with character and personality held, as has been previously observed, a fascination for Shirley Jackson; for her, houses — at least her fictional houses — were like people. They not only reflected the egos and foibles of their original owners, who often had unusual tastes, but they also exerted a mysterious force of their own. As a busy writer, mother, and housewife, she had little time for sight-seeing; but she did spend some time in Salem, Massachusetts, "exploring old witch houses"; and, when Mr. Hyman was involved with writing about Flannery O'Connor, a project involving a trip to Milledgeville, Georgia, Miss Jackson took the opportunity to visit old Southern mansions.

All three of the novels discussed in this chapter, *The Sundial* (1958), *The Haunting of Hill House* (1959), and *We Have Always Lived in the Castle* (1962), are novels of suspense in which setting, a house, is a primary factor. All three have offbeat plots: *The Sundial*, a fantasy, is a modern Gothic novel; *The Haunting* Miss Jackson referred to as a good "ghost story"; and *Castle* is the character study of a young psychopathic mass murderess, a book that might also have been included with the psychological novels. Of the three, *The Sundial* received the least favorable critical reviews; but, sixteen years after its publication, it is still a favorite with the reading public. For instance, an examination of checkout dates on a particular copy of *The Sundial* in a city library disclosed that the book had been checked out twenty-four times during a recent ten-month period. Moreover, *The Haunting*, which became a movie, and *Castle*, made into a Broadway play, received good reviews and remained popular books.

I *The Sundial*

Although much of Miss Jackson's interest in structure was inherited from her architect ancestors in California, her study of eighteenth-century English literature — reflecting the interest of that age in Gothic architecture — undoubtedly inspired her. She loved eighteenth-century novels and that included the newer genre, the Gothic novel, which had been introduced into England through Horace Walpole's *The Castle of Otranto*. One of the chief characteristics of the Gothic novel — which evolved from a renewed interest in the medieval — is the use of the dark and mysterious castle or country home as a functional setting for the unusual events in which it plays an important role; and such is the house in *The Haunting*.

For *The Sundial*, Miss Jackson chooses a mysterious home, except that it is not dark and gloomy. The first Mr. Halloran, suddenly finding himself immensely wealthy, "could think of nothing better to do with his money than set up his own world." His house was to contain everything: objects of beauty, rooms "endlessly decorated and adorned." Since Mr. Halloran is a methodical man, the right wing of the house has twenty windows, as does the left wing, with a great door in the middle; on the second floor, there are forty-two windows across and, on the third floor, the same. One hundred and six thin pillars hold up the ballustrade on the left; the same on the right. All items are balanced perfectly except for the sundial, which is set badly off-center on the lawn.

Many of the features of the house and estate, including the sundial, are ones that had been popular in eighteenth-century England. For example, Miss Jackson includes a grotto; and Alexander Pope's garden at Twickenham had a grotto, as did the grounds of Horace Walpole's famous rebuilt, Gothic mansion "Strawberry Hill." The grotto in the novel turns out to be a disappointment to Mr. Halloran, for it is damp and not at all romantic; and the swans belonging to the lake, overlooked by the grotto (also a necessary part of the scheme), are ill-tempered, ready to attack visitors. Therefore, Fanny (Mr. Halloran's daughter) automatically barricades the opening of the cave when she visits it again after some years; she remembers the vicious swans.

The plan for the formal gardens is also reminiscent of eighteenth-century gardens: besides the ornamental lake, there is a pagoda, a maze — the solution to which hinges on the name Anna, Mr. Halloran's wife, and a rose garden with marble statues. A summer house, built like a temple, echoes the eighteenth-century craze for Chinese architecture. The walls of the house are painted soft colors with scenes of "nymphs and satyrs sporting among flowers and trees."

The house in this novel has a unique function in that it serves as a
Noah's Ark for its inhabitants. The Halloran mansion, the only structure that is to survive the terrible storm signaling the end of civilization, allows its chosen few to become the pioneers of a new world.
The story begins realistically but develops into a fantasy. The reader
does not know until the end of the book (and not even then) whether
or not the total pronouncement of destruction has come about and
whether or not, when they open the doors after the storm, there will
indeed be a beautiful new creation. Up to that point, the predictions
seem to have come true.

The story begins mysteriously with the funeral of Lionel Halloran
and with the accusation that his mother had pushed him downstairs
so that she could become sole owner of the mansion. Shortly after
Lionel's funeral, Aunt Fanny receives warnings from her dead father
that the world is coming to an end and that they must prepare for the
event since only the persons in the house will survive. Gradually,
everyone begins to believe the predictions and to prepare for the
event. Within the safety of the house, the power-play of Mrs.
Halloran, the head of the household who decides to be a queen in
the new world, ends with her murder on the eve of the storm. The
murderer is never exposed, but the reader suspects Mrs. Halloran's
granddaughter, ten-year-old Fancy. Greed and ambition mark the
men, women, and child of the Halloran family as basically evil and
as destroyers of any new world they could ever hope to inherit. As
with "The Lottery," the countryside surrounding the house is essentially a small New England community; nevertheless, the community itself could be almost anywhere in the so-called civilized
world. Man is flawed wherever he exists, and he lives with greed,
ambition, hypocrisy, cruelty, and prejudice. But a few characters in
Miss Jackson's stories and novels seem to contain a preponderance of
good; and they, therefore, remain the only hope for mankind. In the
Sundial, such a character is Gloria, a young friend of the family, who
is able to see visions of the future and to describe vaguely to the
others what is to happen.

Besides the mysterious mansion, one finds in the early Gothic tales
an overdose of symbolism and startling events that serve as
foreshadowings of the great mystery about to be unfolded. These
elements, which underline the mystery and build suspense, are
found in The Sundial. At least one critic deplored the superfluity of
symbols, for, from a modern point of view, their excessive use might
well be considered a weakness of the novel. In The Sundial, though a

fantasy, the narrative is treated realistically and, often, humorously. Here, as in many Gothic novels, there are mysterious deaths; and no explanations are given for supernatural events or unusual occurrences. In Walpole's *Castle of Otranto* the servants believe they see in the library a giant arm — belonging to the huge statue in the courtyard, symbolizing unrest on the part of the original owner of the castle — and in the Halloran mansion a snake suddenly appears from nowhere and slides across the living room floor as the family sits horrified.

Aunt Fanny has just disclosed a pronouncement made during the reappearance of her dead father, a warning about danger but that he would protect the house. No one will listen until the snake appears. "Blasphemy," Essex says politely to Mrs. Halloran. "Sent, no doubt, by the noble ghost you were mocking. You should pay more attention to what you are saying." And, when Mrs. Halloran says that she will have the room fumigated, Aunt Fanny says, "You won't find the snake. . . . It was shining, full of light. You won't find it." As the author later comments, "Not one of the people around Aunt Fanny believed her father's warning, but they were all afraid of the snake."[1] In *The Castle of Otranto*, the portrait of the wronged ancestor suddenly falls from the wall; here, in *The Sundial*, after another of Aunt Fanny's revelations, the glass of the great picture window shatters "soundlessly from top to bottom."

And, early one morning as Aunt Fanny and ten-year-old Fancy walk through the misty garden, they see a strangely dressed man on a ladder, who is apparently trimming one of the hedges. Later, however, Mrs. Halloran tells them that no gardeners have been hired yet to cut the hedges. In another instance, when Aunt Fanny is lost in the mist of the garden, she is disturbed to find the marble statues strangely warm. Easier to explain, perhaps, are the little voodoo dolls, images of Mrs. Halloran stuck with pins; and Mrs. Halloran's hankie, which is discovered near the summer house tied around the neck of a dead garter snake. Although no clues are given, one suspects that little Fancy, her grandmother's heir, may be the culprit.

In fact, the story begins with a scene between Fancy and her mother, young Mrs. Halloran (Maryjane), just after the funeral of Fancy's father Lionel. As they speak of Maryjane's mother-in-law, the elder Mrs. Halloran, Maryjane says, "Maybe she will drop dead on the doorstep? Fancy, dear, would you like to see Granny drop dead on the doorstep?" Fancy answers, "Yes, Mother." Then to

Maryjane's comment, "I am going to pray for it as long as I live," Fancy replies: "Shall I push her? . . . Like she pushed my daddy?" (3).

The older Mrs. Halloran has achieved her wish whether by fair means or foul; but the reader, who wonders if she murdered her own son to gain possession of the house that she has always wanted, assumes that she has. Nevertheless, as in many of the short stories, the ambiguities and scattered bits of information do not allow the reader to be certain. One is certain, however, of the ruthlessness under the ladylike, even pleasant exterior of Mrs. Orianna Halloran. Mr. Halloran, builder of the house, now long dead, had been her father-in-law; for she was a servant in the house when she married his son Richard. At present, Richard is in a wheelchair; and whatever ailment struck him has affected his brain so that he is often childish and has losses of memory. He has a nurse to feed him and to read to him. And, if Orianna Halloran is not exactly a loving wife, she is, at least, pleasant and polite.

Of the other persons living in the house, Aunt Fanny, Richard's sister and the daughter of the builder, despises her sister-in-law; and, though Fanny is continually conscious of being a lady, she cannot resist casting snide remarks now and then about Orianna's lack of a suitable background. The remainder of the household — as the story opens — consists of Essex, a cultured young man in his thirties, who has supposedly been retained to catalogue the ten thousand books in the library but who has become, one is led to believe, the lover of Mrs. Orianna Halloran. There is also Miss Ogilvie, pale, colorless, old-maidish, who has the proper upbringing and who is governess to Fancy. Four years previously, before Richard Halloran had become ill, he had been sending little notes to Miss Ogilvie. Essex had uncovered this information for Mrs. Halloran; and, although no other mention is made of the intrigue, it is quite possible that Orianna has been responsible for Richard's resultant illness in her determination to see that no one else is to usurp her house. And now that Lionel, her son, is gone, she is complete mistress of the domain. As a result, she sees herself as a queen; and, in this capacity, she has resolved to send the others away since she no longer needs them. Fancy is to stay with her to inherit the kingdom; her daughter-in-law, Maryjane, is to go back to the city and the public library where Lionel found her — but she is to receive a suitable cash settlement. Miss Ogilvie is to be sent to some nice, quiet, fashionable boarding home; and Essex is to be relieved of his duties with a small stipend to start him on "some scholarly pursuit." Aunt Fanny is to be sent to the tower — a remote apartment that was to have been an observatory. And Richard, her husband, is to be allowed to stay, for which he is grateful.

As is evident, in addition to eighteenth-century elements, Miss Jackson has chosen to include touches of the Elizabethan era through the characters Orianna, an apparent counterpart to Queen Elizabeth, who often sent victims to the tower, and Essex, her courtier. Mrs. Halloran thinks of Essex in that role when she has forgotten for a moment that he is being sent away: "Poor Essex, unable to comprehend that the essence of the good courtier must be insecurity."

While the unhappy victims consider their uncertain futures, Aunt Fanny, in shock, arrives from the garden with the news that she has just been visited by her dead father; he has warned that there will be "black fire and red water and the earth turning and screaming," but that in the house there is no danger; therefore, they must stay in the house. This pronouncement indicates that the world is to be destroyed but that the people in the house will be saved, and this message everyone makes light of until the snake appears. Aunt Fanny wholeheartedly believes in the revelations; and, after more messages, Mrs. Orianna Halloran, wanting to take no chances, also accepts them as truth. The others are easily persuaded when it is agreed that everyone is to remain at the house. The idea of being chosen to enter a new world is to them both frightening and exciting. Mr. Halloran asks his nurse to stop reading him weekly magazines and begin on *Robinson Crusoe*. Planning begins.

At this point, old friends of Mrs. Halloran, a Mrs. Willow and her two daughters, arrive for a visit. Still another visitor is young Gloria Desmond, whose father, a cousin of Mrs. Halloran's, has asked permission for Gloria to stay with her while he is hunting in Africa. A later acquisition is a stranger whom Aunt Fanny meets in town and invites to the house; although she knows nothing about him, she calls him "captain" and is willing for him to share their future. It has occurred to the women in the group that males will be needed for procreation.

Aunt Fanny has taken charge of ordering supplies from the nearby city: canned foods, medicines, tools, guns, eight bicycles, rope, axes, shovels, overshoes, sunglasses, umbrellas, a carton of tennis balls, suntan lotion, salted nuts in cans, paper napkins, cartons of cigarettes, four cartons of toilet paper, etc. The only books to be included are a *Boy Scout Handbook*, an encyclopedia, Fancy's French grammar book (lest she forget her French), and a *World Almanac*.

For some time, no one is able to determine the date of the destruction, since Aunt Fanny's father has not supplied that information. Finally, the resourceful Mrs. Willow suggests a fortune-telling device from her youth: a young virgin (Gloria is elected) is to look into a mirror that has been placed flat on a table and on which a bit of olive oil has been poured; and she is to look into the mirror as if it were an open window. On her first try, Gloria does see a white rock, then black and red colors that burn her eyes; finally, she seems to see the house and then a large bird, "red and blue and green, like jewels." When the hideous smiling bird with its sharp nose and red eyes seems to be coming straight toward her, Gloria covers her eyes in terror. Mrs. Willow pats her shoulder reassuringly while Aunt Fanny says: " 'I'm sure that it was my father. . . . I know that it was my father, and he has come to see if we are mindful of his instructions. . . . Don't be afraid. . . . That was my father you saw. . . . He was always a very strict man, but good to his children. If I had been in your place, Gloria, I should have said something, or at least made some gesture to show you recognized him. Because of course he has his feelings, too' " (75).

There are many humorous sections, most of them connected with Aunt Fanny's strange logic and complete faith in her father. Several days pass before Gloria can be persuaded to look into the mirror again. When she does, Mrs. Willow asks her what she sees on a certain date, each time pushing the day farther ahead. On August 28, Gloria sees their group sitting and talking in the drawing room. On August 29, they seem to be dancing on the lawn; but, on August 30, since there is only darkness, they reason that this is the date for the end of the world.

Mrs. Halloran has cautioned the group to say nothing of the coming phenomenon to the servants or to any one else in the village. And, when the trucks begin unloading the cartons upon cartons of supplies, she trusts that people will think only that Aunt Fanny's mind has suddenly slipped into imbecility. On a venture into town, however, with Aunt Fanny, Miss Ogilvie makes some strange comments to the clerk at the drugstore. The young man, seeming to understand, says that his mother belongs to a group such as Miss Ogilvie's, The True Believers; and they, too, speak of judgment day and get messages from the spirit world. Miss Ogilvie, disturbed, reports to Aunt Fanny that there may be ten more people joining them. One of the most humorous incidents in the book is the visit from the representatives of The True Believers. Mrs. Orianna Halloran receives them in the ballroom:

> The leader of The True Believers was a lady of indeterminate shape, but vigorous presence, perhaps fortified by the silent support of Liliokawani, queen in Egypt. She swept into Mrs. Halloran's ballroom with the air of one testing the floor for durability; she was wearing a purple dress which presumably fit her, and a fur boa of color and fluff. Behind her came a second, also purple, lady, whose hair was red, and, behind her a man whose determined majesty was most convincing; he had magnificent hair, which suffered little by comparison with the leader's fluffy fur, and he wore, perhaps out of deference, a white waistcoat. At the very last came a withered little lady, peering. (100)

As it turns out, the two groups cannot get together since The True Believers (getting ready to go to Saturn via a spaceship that is to come for them sometime at the end of August or early September) are not allowed to eat meat, drink alcoholic beverages, or be in contact with metal of any sort — including zippers; and Mrs. Halloran tells them softly but firmly that her own group is not qualified to join theirs. When they have gone, she says to Essex: " . . . I will *not* have space ships landing on my lawn. Those people are perfectly capable of sending their saucers just anywhere, with no respect for private property. I want all the gates checked, today . . ." (104).

Despite the touches of humor, the proceedings and the attitudes of the persons in the house are serious. In order to make room for the supplies and yet not attract unnecessary attention, one group places the boxes on the library shelves while another group carries out and burns the books. Essex is the only one to have misgivings about the book-burning; but he, too, complies with the wishes of the group, who must be concerned now with the basic necessities for survival. As Aunt Fanny reminds them, they do not know what the condition of the earth will be on the morning after the destruction when they finally leave the house and step out into the new world. Gloria's visions from the mirror have shown green fields and flowers, but they cannot be sure.

As a farewell gesture, Mrs. Orianna Halloran wishes to give a celebration for the village. Since she cannot call it a farewell party, she will call it a golden-wedding anniversary. When Maryjane and Aunt Fanny object to her disregard for truth and when Mrs. Willow points out that Orianna could not have been married more than twenty-eight years, she is not disturbed: " 'The village,' Mrs. Halloran said, 'will not care particularly how many years Richard and I have been married — beyond marveling at my youthful appearance — and I am sure that my good friends will not quarrel with my desire to do honor, one last time, to the husband of my choice and . . .' she hesitated, '. . . the joy of my life. In other words, I choose to hold a celebration, and I do not care how it may be justified; the burning of the books in the barbecue pit has put me in mind of a public barbecue — ' 'A witch-burning?' said Gloria, but no one heard her" (169).

A public celebration is set, therefore, for the last evening, August 29, and it is to be held on the lawns of the big house. For the occasion, Orianna says, she will sit on the terrace under a gold canopy: " 'I want my people to have their last remembrance of me — if they have time to give me a thought at all — as truly regal; I plan to wear a crown' " (172). Mrs. Willow tells her that she will look like a fool; but Mrs. Halloran, who has many plans for the future, replies: " 'You have not perceived then, Augusta, that I wear a crown on August twenty-ninth to emphasize my position after August thirtieth. . . . I shall probably never remove the crown, until I hand it on to Fancy' " (174). Mrs. Halloran sees herself as ruler of the new world, and she intends to establish her claim early so that there will be no question.

Accordingly, to Fanny's annoyance, she prepares and distributes a list of instructions concerning the last two days and the day after the holocaust. Among other rules are: no person is to leave the house after four o'clock in the afternoon of August thirtieth; the servants and household staff are to leave by noon of that day; all persons in the house are to begin work immediately to board up windows and doors and cover them with blankets; no one is to leave the drawing room during the night of August 30; when morning arrives, Mrs. Halloran will lead the way outside while the others follow in solemn procession; also, no one except Mrs. Halloran may wear a crown. There is included the warning that mates will be assigned by Mrs. Halloran: "Indiscriminate coupling will be subject to severe punishment." Most damning of all is the stipulation that "On the First Day, and thereafter, wanton running, racing, swimming, play of various kinds, and such manifestations of irresponsibility will of course not be permitted. It is expected that all members of the party will keep in mind their positions as inheritors of the world, and conduct themselves accordingly. A proud dignity is recommended, and extreme care lest offense be given to supernatural overseers who may perhaps be endeavoring to determine the fitness of their choice of survivors" (192). "Father, what have you done to me?" asks Fanny as she reads Orianna's rules.

As August draws to an end, the weather becomes strange; there are unusual storms and strange phenomena. The atmosphere in the house becomes tense, but it is time to prepare for the big neighborhood celebration, for which each person has his assignment. The lawn is decorated with Japanese lanterns, a tent is set up for the serving of the champagne, and the beef roasts sizzle in the barbecue pit. Orianna sits regally in a gold-cloth dress, wearing her crown; and she smiles as her guests come to greet her. The evening is a success, for, at its end, even the village maiden ladies, critical of all they see, are gay with champagne, dancing, and the general merriment. Considering the catastrophic event taking place the next day, of which none of the villagers is aware, the reader is reminded of biblical days of judgment upon wicked populations — but the reader, himself, is in suspense, not knowing how all this is to end. At one point near the close of the evening, Miss Ogilvie, stung with conscience and champagne, tries to plead publicly for the people to remain, that otherwise they will die. A silence follows this announcement, which is ended when Mrs. Halloran says, "Music"; the orchestra begins again, and the awkward moment is over.

During the night, the wind rises and with ever increasing intensity continues throughout the day. The rose garden is swept bare; statues fall; the swans cower on the floor of the grotto. By noon, Mrs. Halloran has sent the servants back to the city. Then the work begins — the covering of windows with blankets, the moving of furniture against doors. The upper floors must suffer for lack of equipment and manpower. Candles are needed for the time the electricity fails, Essex reminds them. All available containers have been filled with water. By three o'clock, most of the work is finished, and " . . . most of their original apprehension had faded into a kind of grim humor. They had done all they could; they were almost used to the crash of the wind against the sides of the house; they were excited and festive, with a kind of picnic air" (235).

Mrs. Halloran has instructed them to go to their rooms to dress for the coming event; at four, they are to meet in the drawing room from which no one is to leave for the remainder of the night. As Miss Jackson describes the proceedings: "The lights went out at last while

they were dressing, and there was so much noise of laughter and running from one room to another and remarks shouted down the dark
hallways that it was difficult to hear even the wind, much less the
sound of Mrs. Halloran going down the staircase. At any rate, they
all appeared considerably surprised when, gathering with their
candles upon the wide landing, festively dressed, eager and excited
beneath WHEN SHALL WE LIVE IF NOT NOW? they saw, all at
once, Mrs. Halloran lying in her golden gown, crumpled at the foot
of the great staircase" (237 - 38).

Mrs. Halloran is dead. " 'I expect somebody pushed her down the
stairs,' Mrs. Willow said. . . . 'Live by the sword, die by the sword.' "
After some moments of confusion and helpless comments from the
bystanders, Fancy suddenly remembers her crown and runs down
the stairs to take it from her grandmother's head. " '*My* crown,
now,' Fancy said, pleased" (239). When the question eventually
arises about what they are to do with Mrs. Halloran's body, Aunt
Fanny suggests that she be put outside; and the others agree. With
some effort, Essex and the captain undo the barricade of the great
door and half drag, half carry Orianna against the strong wind
currents across the lawn to the sundial. There they place her in a sitting position next to it, overlooking the lawns. They hurry back to
the house to wait out the long night: " 'My.' Mrs. Willow stretched,
and sighed. 'It's going to be a long wait,' she said. 'The first thing I
will do,' Essex said to Gloria, 'is to make *you* a crown of flowers' "
(245). With those words the book ends.

Because Gloria has seen images of green fields and flowers, one
may assume that that is, perhaps, the future that they will find.
Unlike the usual murder story or the typical Gothic tale, the death is
not accounted for; and no one is to pay the penalty.Each of the
characters has reason to dislike Orianna and might have "pushed"
her; but the most likely candidate is Fancy, who did not hate her
grandmother, but who inherited her grandmother's ambition and
ruthlessness. The crown has caught her imagination, and several
times Orianna has unwittingly told her that the entire domain is to
be hers when her grandmother dies. An enigma and often a liar,
Fancy enjoys teasing people weaker than herself: "Not a servant, or
an animal, or any child in the village near the house, would willingly
go near her."

Seventeen-year-old Gloria, closest in age to Fancy, is the only person in whom she seems to confide. She has told Gloria that she is
tired of playing with dolls; she wants to see the real world; and now

she will never have a chance to do the things about which she has dreamed. In reply to Gloria's comment about the importance of safety and security, Fancy answers:" 'Who wants to be *safe*, for heaven's sakes? . . . I'd rather live in a world full of other people, even dangerous people. I've been *safe* all my life' " (184 - 85). Despite, or because of, her youth and inexperience with worldly affairs, Fancy has an insight that the others lack. She asks Gloria what makes people think that they will be any happier or more peaceful in the new world than they have been in this one: " '. . . you all want the whole world to be changed so *you* will be different. But I don't suppose people get changed any by just a new world. And anyway that world isn't any more real than this one' "(165). Fancy realizes that people will not be different because their environment has changed.

It is interesting to observe that none of the characters, although faced with possible destruction, looks to God for comfort. In fact, one has the strange feeling that Fanny's father may turn out to be the supreme ruler of the new land. Fanny's father is finally exposed as an unsympathetic and cruel man; but, for the reader, he is no longer ominous. Miss Jackson's humor has destroyed his image by identifying him with the grotesque, smiling bird that Gloria sees during a séance.

Ironically, had Mrs. Halloran been permitted to control the new world with her rules and restrictions, her "people" would have been less free than before. People, Miss Jackson says, create their own hells. Except for Gloria, the most honest and noble person of the group, the survivors are selfish, unhappy, deeply flawed individuals who, given a clean slate and a chance for another beginning, would ruin it all again. There is irony in this realization as there is irony throughout the book. Mrs. Halloran, having spent years acquiring full possession of the house, is murdered by (one supposes) the only person whom she trusts to carry on after she is gone. Her plans for becoming a real queen are shattered sooner, perhaps, through acquisition of the pseudo-crown which Fancy sees as a new toy.

In the initial irony, the first Mr. Halloran has sought to create his own world, principally for his young wife; but three months after they move in, she dies, never having seen the gardens, the grotto, the lake, or the sundial. In fact, nothing turns out as planned: the grotto is damp; the swans are unfriendly; the sundial is off-center. The reader finds irony in Aunt Fanny's references to her father as noble, righteous, and wise; for one learns from the accounts of the villagers that he was, instead, egoistic, vicious, and ungodly. That *he* should be an instrument of survival for the chosen group is also ironic. Despite Aunt Fanny's seeming attachment to her father, one discovers that she has had a singularly empty, loveless life; for, after the death of her mother, she had received little affection or attention from her father.

Also ironic is the library situation — ten thousand books are sacrificed for the containers of supplies, indicating that education and learning are not to be valued in the new environment. The accumulated wisdom of the ages counts for little and is, apparently, of little use in basic survival. The hardy indispensables turn out to be the *Boy Scout Handbook*, the *World Almanac*, and the encyclopedia. In addition, irony exists in the hypocrisy of the village people, especially the inhumane Misses Inverness, who are so proud of their genteel upbringing. When Essex, at the garden party, fantasizes a past for Miss Ogilvie by saying that she was violated as a child by a band of Comanche Indians, these ladies, who have been her friends for several years, are shocked that they were not informed of this blemish on her character which now makes her unsuitable as an associate. Much champagne later, after Essex tells them of the captain's past as a murderer of old women (sex crimes, it is assumed), Miss Deborah Inverness clutches the captain's arm and follows him about until he manages to elude both her and the local schoolteacher.

There is irony in the application of the two central maxims on the Halloran estate: the most prominent indoor motto in black Gothic letters touched with gold over the arched window at the landing on the great stairway is WHEN SHALL WE LIVE IF NOT NOW?; and the inscription on the sundial is WHAT IS THIS WORLD? The first Mr. Halloran was so pleased with the idea of maxims that he would have placed one in each room if the architect had not dissuaded him. Even so, there are several inscriptions in various strategic spots; for instance, on the inside wall of the grotto are the words, "Fear no more the heat of the sun." According to the author, when the tension between Mr. Halloran and the principal architect became unbearable, the architect's young nephew, who had a master's in English literature from Columbia University, suggested a more poetic wording of the old saws. Therefore, the saying "You can't take it with you" became "When shall we live if not now?" Orianna thought she was to take all of her possessions with her into the new world, the principal possession being the house; but, ironically, the object she has spent the major part of her life acquiring remains for the others while she goes alone to a world where no belongings are allowed or needed. The young man, by the way, who had hoped for aid from Mr. Halloran to advance his career of writing plays in blank verse, was offered by him a position as file clerk, which he took; he later became chief clerk and then got married.

The other major inscription, on the sundial, was suggested to Miss Jackson by poet Howard Nemerov, but in the story it is provided by some imaginative soul in Philadelphia where the sundial was ordered. Mrs. Halloran has never liked the wording, but Essex has several times obligingly recited to her the Chaucerian lines of which it is a part:

> What is this world?
> What asketh man to have?
> Now with his love,
> Now in his cold grave,
> All alone, withouten any companye!

As it happens, Mrs. Halloran, all alone, is finally set at rest next to the sundial.

The question What is this world? has in one way or another been the subject of conversation for several of the characters. To Gloria, in her seventeen-year-old experience, the world within the Halloran mansion is real; the world outside is fake; but the cause for her cynicism is not known: "*Nothing* out there is real. Everything is made out of something else, and everything is made to look like something else, and it all comes apart in your hands. The people aren't real, they're nothing but endless copies of each other, all looking just alike, like paper dolls, and they live in houses full of artificial things and eat imitation food — " (185).

To Fancy, who has never experienced any world outside the Halloran walls, the real world is there: dancing and boys, going to parties, pretty dresses, movies, and football games. The first Mr. Halloran had intended to create his own world, but the material world crumbled for him when his wife died, and nothing was ever the same thereafter. To Aunt Fanny, the real world has always been linked to childhood memories before their family moved to the mansion and when her mother was still alive. To Essex, Miss Ogilvie, and

Mrs. Willow, the Halloran mansion is as real and secure a world as they can hope for; it is their haven from the poverty that has been their lot in life.

As to reality:

> "Reality," Essex said. . . . "What is real, Aunt Fanny?"
> "The truth," said Aunt Fanny at once.
> "Comfort," said Mrs. Willow. . . . Julia laughed. "Essex," she said, "what is real?" . . . "I am real," he said. "I am not at all sure about the rest of you." . . .
> "Well, reality," Mrs. Willow said finally, "all it means is money. A roof over your head, of course, and a little something three times a day and maybe a drop to drink. But mostly money. . . ." (66 - 67)

The world to which they are going is frightening because it is unknown, and there is no choice involved; but it is also exciting.

The sundial, a focal point and reminder of the transience of man, is as imperfect as the characters are. As an object, it is the only feature that mars what is otherwise architectural perfection. Earlier, as Mrs. Halloran studies it, she thinks: " . . . without it the lawn would be empty. It is a point of human wickedness; it is a statement that the human eye is unable to look unblinded upon mathematical perfection. I am earthly. . . . I must look at the sundial like anyone else. I am not inhuman; if the sundial were taken away, I, too, would have to avert my eyes until I saw imperfection, a substitute sundial — perhaps a star" (14 - 15). However, one has the feeling that, even if the other objects of the landscape were destroyed, the sundial would remain undisturbed.

The range of critical response to *The Sundial* was wide and varied, but most reviewers were essentially puzzled by it and offered both negative and positive comments. No one seemed wholly overjoyed with the book, although many agreed that it was entertaining. Edmund Fuller (*Chicago Sunday Tribune*, February 23, 1958) states: "It would take a rash man to assert dogmatically what Shirley Jackson is up to in any of the novels generated by her unique talent. *The Sundial* will be many things to many readers, but for all of them it should be entertaining, absorbing and disturbing. . . . As a type of the dream experience, which is the character of the book's patterns, it is marvelously imagined."[2]

As noted before, Miss Jackson gets an "A" for her storytelling abilities; no one denies her talent, but not everyone agrees with her choice of theme or plot. Harvey Swados asks in the *New Republic*, (March 3, 1958): "Why is it that the book finally leaves such a small impression? For one reader it is primarily because while Miss Jackson is an intelligent and clever writer, there rises from her pages the cold fishy gleam of a calculated and carefully expressed contempt for the human race."[3] And Peter Girvin in the *New York Herald Tribune Book Review* (February 16, 1958), puzzled as to the point of it all, says:

It is possible, usually, to make a reasonably safe guess as to why any technically skilled and intellectually prescient writer has undertaken to write a particular novel. With Shirley Jackson's *The Sundial* it is not that easy. My own guesses range all the way from a shocked surmise that Miss Jackson's strange story is a corrosive satire on the absurdity of simple faith in a space-obsessed, materialistic-minded modern world, to a suspicion that she is merely engaged in putting her two high-stepping thoroughbreds — literary finesse and macabre fancy — through their distinguished paces. . . . No one who has read Miss Jackson's other works needs telling how perfectly she has here captured her foolish human flies in the amber of her consummate skill. But whether *The Sundial* be a romp, a phantasy, or a poker-faced satire is for you to say.[4]

Mr. Girvin has not considered that the book need not be any *one* of these types exclusively. Rather, it seems to be all *three:* a romp *and* a fantasy *and* a poker-faced satire. It is a romp in the playful attitude Miss Jackson often takes toward her characters in the humorous escapades in which they become involved and in the tone in which they are described; in fact, the novel could be seen as a huge shaggy-dog story. In addition, the book is definitely a fantasy; events take place that leap the bounds of credulity, and the strange symbols and foreshadowings are not realistic. It is not likely, either, that the world could come to an end in this ridiculous fashion or that these unlikely candidates would be the chosen few, except, of course, in some inspired cosmic joke. Besides being a romp and a fantasy, the book is a serious satire on mankind, for the follies, vices, and weaknesses of these characters are exposed for all to see, and these people represent all mankind.

William Peden in *The Saturday Review* (March 8, 1958) also has praise and some adverse criticism. The praise is for her storytelling abilities; the negative criticism is for her seeming preoccupation with symbols: "From the very outset *The Sundial* is alive with the peculiar magic which Shirley Jackson has conjured in earlier novels

like *Hangsaman* and *The Bird's Nest.* . . . In addition to being a
first-class story teller, she has always been concerned with the conflict between good and evil in a world deplorably deficient in common sense, kindness, and magnanimity, in the Aristotelian sense.
The Sundial is no exception."[5] Peden, who lists a few of the many
symbols Miss Jackson includes in the novel, believes that the
superfluity of symbols, "tends to blunt the edge of Miss Jackson's
story." The criticism is just, for the reader becomes confused by the
many symbols. Perhaps the answer is that the author was treating
the story as a Gothic novel, in which there are symbols galore, all
guaranteed to add mystery and suspense to the atmosphere. The
modern reader, however, has no patience with mysteries that appear
to be artificial manipulations.

Perhaps one of the most interesting reviews is that of Jean
Holzhauer (*Commonweal*, April 4, 1958), who contended that the
work was actually an allegory of the Catholic Church:

Many interpretations are possible; one, a little more than possible, is the
equation of the Halloran realm with its wealth, enclosure, certainty of
superiority and survival, revelation in one branch of the family and
organization in the other (with the two branches genteely at war),
sycophants, rebellious rational minds — and the Catholic Church. In this
reading Mrs. Halloran becomes a Mother Church figure; the warm marble
statues in the garden remnants of paganism; Aunt Fanny in her precedence
as a Halloran and her bare tolerance of Orianna, the Old Testament
prophets; Mrs. Halloran's ghostly father-in-law, the voice of God, her more
or less invisible, always manipulable husband, that spouse of whom Mrs.
Halloran is the bride. Mrs. Willow becomes something like Secularism,
limited and crassly envying the Halloran empire weak and vulnerable to
confusion. And surely the despised Miss Inverness, daughter of the agnostic
whom God mentioned with affection, becomes the Protestant sects.[6]

Miss Holzhauer points out also that this view would indicate that the
novel is anti-Catholic. She realizes, apparently, that much of the
satire is too broad and too general to be an attack solely on the
Church. Needless to say, it is doubtful that Miss Jackson had such an
interpretation in mind.

Norman Shrapnel (*Manchester Guardian*, August 19, 1958),
another reviewer who praised the novel and yet thought that it fell
short of its goal, says in part: "It doesn't quite come off, but Shirley
Jackson's audacious attempt at a high-level horror comic is one of
the most versatile things of its kind, since the Ingoldsby Legends and

quite the most remarkable book in this summer batch."[7] If the book does fail, perhaps the fault lies with the difficulty of sympathizing with the protagonist, Mrs. Halloran. Except for Gloria, there is no person with whom the reader can identify; for the characters — although well drawn — are not nice people. Despite interest in an engrossing story and curiosity as to its outcome, one does not become emotionally involved.

II   The Haunting of Hill House

The inspiration to write a ghost story came to Miss Jackson, according to her account in the article "Experience and Fiction," as she was reading a book about a group of nineteenth-century psychic researchers who rented a haunted house in order to study it and record their impressions of what they had seen and heard for the purpose of presenting a treatise to the Society for Psychic Research. As she recalls: "They thought that they were being terribly scientific and proving all kinds of things, and yet the story that kept coming through their dry reports was not at all the story of a haunted house, it was the story of several earnest, I believe misguided, certainly determined people, with their differing motivations and backgrounds."[8] The story so excited her that she could hardly wait to create her own haunted house and her own people to study it.

Shortly thereafter, she states, on a trip to New York, she saw at the 125th Street station, a grotesque house — one so evil-looking, one that made such a somber impression, that she had nightmares about it long afterward. In response to her curiosity, a New York friend investigated and found that the house, intact from the front, was merely a shell since a fire had gutted the structure, leaving only the frame of the remaining walls. In the meantime, she was searching newspapers, magazines, and books for pictures of suitably haunted-looking houses; and she at last discovered a magazine picture of a house that seemed just right. It looked very much like the hideous building she had seen in New York: ". . . it had the same air of disease and decay, and if ever a house looked like a candidate for a ghost, it was this one." The picture identified the house as being in a California town; consequently, hoping her mother in California might be able to acquire some information about the house, she wrote asking for help. As it happened, her mother was not only familiar with the house but provided the startling information that Miss Jackson's great-grandfather had built it. Apparently, it had stood vacant and deserted for many years until, it was believed, a group of townspeople burned it down. She had been surprised that there were still pictures of the house in circulation.

While seeking the proper house, Miss Jackson did research about ghosts. As she says, she had always been interested in witchcraft and superstition, but she knew little about spirits. Her information came from personal inquiry and the reading of books, especially true ghost stories. No one that she contacted had ever seen a ghost, but most people had the uneasy suspicion that, at some undisclosed time, they just might run into one. After the house had been selected and with the psychic research well under way, the writing went smoothly. Finally, the novel was finished; published in 1959 by the Viking Press, it went through several printings and many foreign editions; it was hailed by critics as one of the best spine-chillers in years.

When Roald Dahl read the book, he contacted Miss Jackson to ask that she consider writing a script for a television show that Emlyn Williams was doing in Britain; for some unknown reason, however, Miss Jackson did not comply with the request. Four years later, on August 21, 1963, the world premiere of the movie version (*The Haunting*) starring Julie Harris and Claire Bloom was held at theaters throughout the Bennington area. Filmed in England, its producer Robert Wise chose as Hill House the historic, centuries' old Ettington Hall near Stratford-on-Avon in Warwickshire. Miss Jackson was pleased with the film, for she felt that the movie retained the original atmosphere of the book.

As she first planned, Miss Jackson peopled her haunted house with individuals who were to record their impressions of the psychic phenomena; but, with the exception of the leader of the group, Dr. Montague, they are not professional scholars. Dr. Montague, a doctor of philosophy, has taken his degree in anthropology, and he hopes to spend some time doing what he enjoys most: analyzing supernatural manifestations. He has, accordingly, rented Hill House and prepared for a summer of enjoyable study. The project has taken a good bit of preparation, for he needs assistants; and proper assistants are not easily found. First, he scans old newspapers for persons connected in some way with abnormal occurrences. After making and then trimming his list, he ends with the names of twelve individuals, each of whom he invites to spend all or part of a summer in a comfortable country house, complete with plumbing, electricity, central heating, and ghosts (although he does not say so).

The purpose of their stay, he says, is to observe and explore the strange stories circulated about the house during its eighty years of existence. Only four persons reply to his invitation; and, of the four, only two come: Eleanor Vance and Theodora (the only name she gives). Luke Sanderson also joins the group, not because he is invited, but because his aunt owns the house; and, wanting to be rid of him for a few weeks, she stipulates that he, as a member of the family, should be included.

As in the other novels there is sparkling conversation and humor interspersed with the more serious and terrifying moments. Each of the persons is sensitive, intelligent, and, to an extent, receptive to the others. Dr. Montague, like Dr. Wright of *The Bird's Nest*, is a bit pompous but able to laugh at himself. Apparently he, like Miss Jackson, is fond of the eighteenth-century novel, for he reads Richardson's novels for relaxation before retiring: *Pamela*, then *Clarissa*, and later *Sir Charles Grandison*.

Eleanor is the main character. Her moment of notoriety had come when she was twelve years old and her sister, eighteen; their father had been dead only a few weeks when suddenly, for no apparent reason, showers of stones fell on their house, rolled down the roof, and broke windows. This phenomenon lasted intermittently for three days until the family went to stay with relatives. Although they returned later to live in the house, there was no recurrence. Neither Eleanor nor her sister had been as much shaken by the experience as by the curiosity and stares of the neighbors. And, as one discovers later, Eleanor had considered her sister responsible for the event, while she, in turn, believed it was Eleanor's doing; but their mother was certain that the neighbors were the culprits. Years later at Hill House Dr. Montague explains this mystery to Eleanor as being, no doubt, the work of poltergeists, the most destructive and least intelligent of spirits.

At the time Eleanor receives the letter from Dr. Montague, she is a plain, rather drab thirty-two years old; her mother, whom she has nursed for twelve years, has been dead for three months; and she is living with her sister and brother-in-law, both of whom she hates, just as she hated her mother. Since the word from Dr. Montague creates the first bit of excitement she has had in years, she is determined to go to Hill House. The other invited guest, Theodora, is a lovely, worldly, temperamental young lady, an artist with her own shop. She has attracted Dr. Montague's notice by her performance in a series of psychic tests in which she had identified correctly an amazing number of cards held up by an unseen but heard assistant. Theo had intended to decline the doctor's invitation, but at a crucial

moment, she and a friend (male or female, one never discovers),
with whom she shares an apartment, have a serious quarrel; consequently, the offer provides a convenient excuse to leave the city for a
few weeks.

Eleanor's trip to Hill House brings her through lonely but
beautiful countryside; and she imagines herself as an occupant of the
various dwellings she sees: a vast home with pillars here — a tiny
cottage there. The reader recognizes Eleanor's need for a home of
her own. These musings are a foreshadowing of her final acceptance
and desire to remain at Hill House. At last she arrives at Hillsdale,
the village six miles from Hill House; the little-used road from the
town is deeply rutted and rocky. As Eleanor travels, one again has
evidence of Miss Jackson's interest in ballads; for lines from a ballad
run through her mind during the last few miles of her journey. The
ballad lines recur throughout the novel, the most insistent of the
lines being "Journeys end in lovers meeting," a phrase that is almost
prophetic but one that does serve to build suspense. Eleanor does
become the center of Luke's attention for a time, before he changes
to the fair Theodora. Taken symbolically, the line could refer to the
acceptance Eleanor finally feels for the spirits of the house. She is
sure that she belongs here, or perhaps it is just that she doesn't
belong anywhere else, for no one else cares. Before Eleanor comes to
the house, she meets at the gate a cantankerous, sullen man named
Mr. Dudley, who finally allows her to pass; later, the reader meets
his wife, the housekeeper; she too is a distinctive character. Eleanor's
first impression is that the house is vile and diseased and that she
should get away from it at once. As the author states:

No human eye can isolate the unhappy coincidence of line and place which
suggests evil in the face of a house, and yet somehow a maniac juxtaposition,
a badly turned angle, some chance meeting of roof and sky, turned Hill
House into a place of despair, more frightening because the face of Hill
House seemed awake, with a watchfulness from the blank windows and a
touch of glee in the eyebrow of a cornice. Almost any house, caught unex-
pectedly or at an odd angle, can turn a deeply humorous look on a watching
person; even a mischievous little chimney, or a dormer like a dimple can
catch a beholder with a sense of fellowship; but a house arrogant and hating,
never off guard, can only be evil. This house, which seemed somehow to
have formed itself, flying together into its own powerful pattern under the
hands of its builders, fitting itself into its own construction of lines and
angles, reared its great head back against the sky without concession to
humanity. It was a house without kindness, never meant to be lived in, not a
fit place for people or for love or for hope. (34 - 35)

This personified description of the house is one of the few passages in which Miss Jackson indulges in a longer, more complicated sentence structure. In it, she makes effective use of nouns and verbs to create a house that is actively evil. The passage foreshadows the ill fortune ahead and, at the same time, builds suspense.

This house, like the Halloran mansion, is a basic ingredient in the plot. Here, the investigation of the house constitutes the purpose for the gathering of the characters. Each of these houses is strange, with a personality of its own. Hill House is dark and unfriendly, and its spirits seem to delight in plaguing the visitors. In both houses, there are odd psychic occurrences: the spirit of Fanny's father appears to guide the inhabitants of the Halloran mansion; at Hill House, unfriendly spirits who are anxious to be rid of the guests have the upper hand. Each of these houses and its grounds seems to be in a separate world, isolated from surrounding communities. Both houses are scenes of mystery, complete with their towers, reminiscent of the abbeys and mansions in Miss Jackson's favorite Gothic novels. In *The Sundial*, Mrs. Halloran threatens to send Fanny to live in the tower; in Hill House, Eleanor tries to climb the stairs leading to the tower and risks her life and Luke's by doing so. As Mrs. Halloran and Fanny love and feel possessive of their home, so Eleanor comes to love and feel at home in Hill House. She does not want to leave; and, when her companions force her to do so, she commits suicide. The builders of both houses were wealthy, autocratic, domineering, and cruel men; each had built the house for his wife, and each had lost that wife early in marriage.

The plot involves not only the relationship of the characters to one another but also the relationship of the characters to the house. Because of loneliness, excessive frustration, and hidden hate, Eleanor is the one most affected and, perhaps, the one who most aggravates the spirits of the house. She looks forward to love and to a meaningful friendship with Theodora and Luke; but, when they become interested in each other, Eleanor is driven to her own resources and to identification with the house. Eventually, she yearns to become one of the spirits of the house and to remain in it forever. Psychologically and emotionally, she has been pushed to the edge of madness and, therefore, slips quietly but gleefully into an acceptance of a new existence.

As in *Hangsaman*, the protagonist suffers a disintegration of the mind; but Eleanor's change is rapid since psychic disturbances cause her to have a series of shocks. Before she accepts the influence of the spirits and is no longer afraid, she goes through a period of great fear and terror. The intervention of Dr. Montague and the others causes the last major crisis in Eleanor's life, for when they insist (for her own good) that she leave the house, she pretends to do so and then drives her car into the big tree in the driveway, the one that had taken another life years before. In this way, she ends her life and becomes one of the spirits. Just before she hits the tree, however, she has a moment of lucidity in which she wonders why she is killing herself and why Theo and Luke don't stop her. But, by then, the crash comes and it is too late.

It is necessary, however, to examine in more detail the events as they occur and the fascination the house has for these people. The reader must accept the possibility of ghosts; for, unless there is such a phenomenon as mass delusion, all members of the party share in seeing and hearing the same manifestations, which are not the product of any one person's imagination. Everyone who arrives at the house is exposed to the set speech of the unsmiling Mrs. Dudley, wife of the caretaker, who becomes a humorous character because of her mechanical inflexibility. Characters such as Mrs. Dudley are a tribute to Miss Jackson's skill in making unique persons of even the less important people. Despite direct questions from the group, Mrs. Dudley gives the same response: "I set dinner on the dining-room sideboard at six sharp. . . . You can serve yourselves. I clear up in the morning. I have breakfast ready for you at nine. That's the way I agreed to do. . . . I don't stay after six. Not after it begins to get dark. So there won't be anyone around if you need help. We couldn't hear you, even in the night. No one could. . . . In the night; in the dark" (43 - 45). As a result, she becomes for the group an object of humor; and only when the doctor's wife arrives for a two-day stay, spending some time in the kitchen, does the reader see that Mrs. Dudley, too, can be a warm, responsive human being, besides being, apparently, an excellent cook.

Luke Sanderson, the remaining guest, meets Theodora and Eleanor for the first time as they come back from a walk near the house. His aunt has said of Luke that he has "the best education, the best clothes, the best taste, and the worst companions of anyone she had ever known." Because they all possess a sense of humor, despite their varying backgrounds, Luke, Eleanor, and Theodora make congenial companions and are willing and cooperative assistants to Dr. Montague. Of the three, Eleanor is the most sensitive, the most alone, and the most vulnerable. Although she and Theo become close friends, she is aware of Theo's selfishness and of her need to be the center of attention.

The house is oddly built — designed on a plan of concentric circles, so that none of the rooms is square nor do the walls form right angles. For this reason, they suppose, none of the doors will stay open unless propped. They agree that they must stay together, for they soon have difficulty finding their way about in the dark, musty, but richly appointed, house. First of all, in their partial exploration of the rooms, they find an odd situation at the entrance of the nursery — a large sub-zero cold spot — for which they can find no explanation. They are excited by the tension, for they know that something will happen, even though the doctor believes that the first night will be a quiet one. As he says, "There is a pattern to these things, as though psychic phenomena were subject to laws of a very particular sort." He would rather talk at some other time about the history of the house, for no one can leave at night. The gates are locked; and the last person, apparently, who tried to leave in darkness (on horseback) eighteen years before, had been killed at the turn in the driveway when his horse bolted and crushed him against the big tree. In light of the events that follow, this mention of the tree is significant. Again, Miss Jackson skillfully builds the suspense by use of careful detail that also lends authenticity to the setting.

The first night in the house is, as the doctor predicted, quiet and peaceful. Eleanor awakens in the morning with a feeling of expectation and well-being; and the others, apparently, feel the same way. At one point Theodora says, "I have a hunch that you ought to go home, Eleanor" (a prophetic statement). Then as the first full day ends, tension increases. "It's like waiting in a dentist's office," Eleanor thinks. The doctor exposes another painful truth when he says, "I think that an atmosphere like this can find out the flaws and faults and weaknesses in all of us, and break us apart in a matter of days." Their only defense, he feels, is to leave; therefore, anyone who begins to feel the adverse influence of the house must promise to leave immediately. The reader is forewarned that trouble is about to begin.

On the second night, Eleanor awakens from a dream, believing that her mother is knocking on the door — when she realizes where she is, she hurries into Theodora's room. Theo, too, is awake. Suddenly the air is very cold, and they hear a noise down the hall. "Something is knocking on the doors," Theodora says. The pounding seems to be going from door to door, making a hollow noise as if something were hitting each with an iron kettle or bar. Just before the noise reaches their door, Eleanor shouts wildly, "Go away!" There is a sudden silence, but the cold becomes more intense, and then the sound begins again. The hammering is at the upper end of the door, higher than humans can reach, Eleanor realizes. Then there are little pattings, "small seeking sounds," as if someone were trying to sneak in. At the same time, the doorknob moves, and then the crashing begins again. Until now the sensations have been auditory, but now they see the door tremble and shake, moving against its hinges. When Eleanor calls again, there is silence for a moment, followed by a giggle which becomes a quiet laugh.

Then they hear Luke and the doctor calling from the stairs, and all is silent again. The crisis seems to be over. Luke says that they were chasing some animal, perhaps a dog, which the doctor had glimpsed running past his door. They followed it down the stairs and outside. They had not heard any sounds in the hall until the girls' voices began. When they gather in Theodora's room, the doctor warns them that they must take precautions, for it would seem that the intention of whatever beings are involved is to separate them.

The experience of the night has left them with a sense of excitement: We are all enjoying ourselves, Eleanor thinks. This excitement, however, troubles the doctor because its intoxicating effect might be dangerous. Moreover, it is the first sign that they have fallen under a spell. Actually, no physical danger exists, he reassures them, for no ghost has ever hurt a human; it is the human who through fear of ghosts does damage to himself. Next, he begins a discourse on the lowest element of the supernatural world, the poltergeists. "Poltergeists are another thing altogether," he says. "They deal entirely with the physical world; they throw stones, they move objects, they smash dishes." He also says that they are "destructive but mindless and will-less; they are merely undirected force." Poltergeists also like to play tricks on people, such as tipping over beds. He indicates that Eleanor's childhood experience was, undoubtedly, due to poltergeists. For the reader, Dr. Montague's informal lecture on the supernatural lends credibility to the atmosphere.

The next manifestation does not wait for night. Luke, gone to the kitchen for a moment, comes back for the others. He has found writing on the wall; from one end of the hall to the other, chalk letters, almost too large to read, plead: HELP ELEANOR COME HOME. Eleanor, almost hysterical, at first suspects Theodora and shouts at her; but the doctor establishes the fact that none of them could have written it. Thereafter, a quiet day and night pass, during which each of them writes an account of what he thinks he has seen and heard so far in Hill House.

The following afternoon, as Eleanor walks into her bedroom, she hears a scream from next door. She runs to find Theodora aghast at what appears to be blood in shaky red letters on the wallpaper above her bed. The words say, HELP ELEANOR COME HOME ELEANOR. Furthermore, the clothes in Theo's closet are torn from the hangers and lie crumpled on the floor; and they are smeared with red. Eleanor tries to comfort her crying friend. She will, she says, share her clothes with Theodora; but she is revolted at the blood that Theo has inadvertently rubbed upon herself. These moments expose the love-hate relationship that exists between the two.

Eleanor is becoming more and more insecure; and, of the influence of the house, she says: "Look. There's only one of me, and it's all I've got. I *hate* seeing myself dissolve and slip and separate so that I'm living in one half my mind, and I see the other half of me helpless and frantic and driven and I can't stop it, but I know I'm not really going to be hurt and yet time is so long and even a second goes on and on and I could stand any of it if I could only surrender . . ." (160).

The others are noticeably concerned over Eleanor's well-being. That night, from the room that had been Theo's, Eleanor and she hear a babbling voice and the room again becomes very cold. Eleanor holds tightly to Theodora's hand in the dark. The low, steady voice becomes a laugh and then the cry of a child, then a shriek. As Eleanor shouts, "Stop it," the lights are suddenly on again; and Theodora, sitting up in bed, asks what the trouble is. With horror, Eleanor wonders whose hand she has been holding. On this note that particular chapter ends. Since most of the chapters end on a note of suspense, the reader is guaranteed to read through without stopping.

Eleanor becomes increasingly lonely; her relationship with Luke that, at first, seemed to be progressing along romantic avenues, is now unsatisfactory. She realizes that he, like Theo, is a thoroughly selfish individual — with the difference that he is looking for a mother. Luke and Theodora now tend to be together more; and when the three go for walks on the grounds, Eleanor is often left by herself while the others are absorbed in each other. One dark evening as Eleanor walks away in anger with Theodora following, they come suddenly upon a garden in bright sunshine with a family picnic therein. Terrified, they both run back to the house.

As comic relief, Miss Jackson introduces, besides Mrs. Dudley, two visitors who come to spend the weekend: one is the doctor's wife, and the other is Arthur Parker, a friend, who is also the headmaster of a boys' preparatory school. Both, as objects of humor, are original and delightful, if not always pleasant characters. Mrs. Montague is as interested in the supernatural as her husband is, but her approach is less scientific. She hopes to project love to the spirits who, she is convinced, are starved for love and recognition. Her main source of communication with the spirit world is by way of automatic writing — planchette; and she immediately takes charge of the search for spirits. No spirits have shown themselves, she says, because her husband's guests are not attuned to the psychic and are not believers. Furthermore, their hostile attitude is, she is sure, bound to scare away the spirits.

The doctor, making no attempt to describe in the presence of his wife the manifestations aleady experienced, becomes a flustered, silent man. As she plans, she sits up for a few hours, and Arthur patrols at regular intervals all night long with a revolver. The irony is that the spirits do not traffic with the newcomers who are seeking them, and Mrs. Montague and Arthur are disgruntled. The reader can appreciate the humor of the situation, for the spirits, like contrary children, appear when and to whom they please; and neither the love approach nor the crude tactics of Mrs. Montague and Arthur seem to interest them.

After she has retired (Mrs. Montague insists upon sleeping in the nursery), the doctor's group gathers in his room. Dr. Montague is worried that Arthur might shoot someone. Then the noises and the pounding begin, and again there is a swift movement as of an animal moving down the hall. It turns out to be a difficult night for Dr. Montague and his guests, who are huddled in the one room: as the furniture sways, the walls move, and the noise continues, they are all badly shaken. Hearing the laughter, Eleanor feels that she can no longer hold out; she will surrender herself to whatever the spirits want of her.

On the other hand, Mrs. Montague and Arthur, who have had a peaceful night, have heard none of the commotion. Again there is the irony and the humor of the spirits' ignoring the two persons who are trying to commune with them. The other guests ignore Mrs. Montague and Arthur also and do not reveal the horrors of the night. Mrs. Montague complains that she did not sleep well because the room was too stuffy, while Arthur says, "Can't understand you . . . letting yourself get all nervy about this place. Sat there all night long with my revolver and not a mouse stirred. Except for that infernal branch tapping on the window. Nearly drove me crazy." Of course, what they do not realize is that the spirits of Hill House seem more saturated with evil than with goodness and love. The annoyance that Mrs. Montague and Arthur complain of may also have been the work of the spirits, who wish not to commune with but to heckle them. The manifestations are present, but they do not recognize them as such.

How much of what happens to the group is imagined is difficult to tell. One might suspect Eleanor of being responsible for some of the strange occurrences since it is she who is singled out for attention. However, the four collectively seem to see and hear the same things, and Eleanor is never really alone in the house. Also puzzling is the significance of the wall messages asking Eleanor to come home. Is *home* the city she left, or is it Hill House and its ghosts who want her to stay? Her gradual acceptance of the house and her desire to surrender herself to it make the latter seem more probable. Because Eleanor is lonely and has no one who cares about her when she returns to the city, she asks to live with Theodora; but Theodora brutally rejects her. "Do you *always* go where you're not wanted?" she asks. "I've never been wanted *anywhere*," Eleanor answers. A key to her present state of mind is revealed when she tells Luke that it was her fault that her mother died: "She knocked on the wall and called me and called me and I never woke up. I ought to have brought her the medicine; I always did before. But this time she called me and I never woke up" (212). One wonders if there is a correspondence in her mind between her mother's knocking on the wall and the spirit's doing so, but one does not know.

The next evening Mrs. Montague is very much upset that the planchette will not speak to her — and the fault lies, she says, with the mocking, sneering unbelievers who are present. Again the reader can appreciate the irony of the situation. Mrs. Montague's lack of sensitivity keeps her from recognizing that the "unbelievers" are the true communicants; nor is she aware of Eleanor's psychic disturbances and their connection with the house. Of course, no one has confided in her, and she is completely oblivious to the drama taking place around her. As Eleanor sits watching Luke and the doctor play chess, she is aware of footsteps in the empty part of the room: someone is singing quietly (another ballad). At the same time, Mrs. Montague asks her, "How would *you* feel if people refused to believe in *you*?" — a condition that does apply to Eleanor since no one seems to believe in her. She ignores the question, realizing with joy that she is the only one in the room who has heard the steps and the singing. Thus, bit by bit, one becomes aware of her increasing attachment to the spirit world and of her increasing isolation from her companions.

That night Eleanor leaves her room and the sleeping Theodora. When she calls "Mother," a voice answers upstairs. She cannot find the voice, but she joyfully runs down to the nursery, feeling compelled to knock on the door. Laughing to herself, she runs down the hallway, knocking on the other doors. No one, she knows, will open a door. Then she hears Theodora calling her name. Since she does not want to be found, she runs to hide; and, finally, hearing everyone in pursuit, runs into the library and climbs the rickety stairs to the tower. Inside the library, she feels at home: "I am home, she thought and stopped in wonder at the thought. I am home, I am home. . . ." Luke rescues her from the swaying, rusty staircase.

At breakfast the next morning, the doctor tells her that she must leave immediately. She tries to tell them that she wants to stay and that she has nowhere else to go. Also, she points out, Theodora must borrow her clothes. Mrs. Montague wants to know why, for in checking the rooms she and Arthur had also checked Theodora's; and the reader (and everyone else) is astounded to learn that there is no longer anything amiss with either the room or the clothes. The havoc in the room earlier with the destruction of Theodora's clothes and its restoration to order are mystic phenomena encountered by the group and another indication that the reader must accept the concept of Miss Jackson's spirit world; for logic alone will not suffice to account for the unusual events.

As they gather on the steps waiting for Eleanor to leave, she thinks, " 'The house was waiting now . . . it was waiting for her; no one else could satisfy it.' " She tells the doctor that the house wants her to stay; and, despite her protests, the group firmly lead her to her car. After the final good-byes, she rebels: "I won't go. Hill House belongs to me!" Laughing to herself, she presses her foot down on the accelerator and turns the wheel so that the car will smash directly into the great tree at the bend in the driveway. At the last moment she thinks, "Why am I doing this? Why don't they stop me?" The tragedy is that the others refuse to see Eleanor's loneliness; they are too much involved with their own problems to want to help.

As in the short stories and in the other novels, the characters are and remain very much alone. Each, concerned with his own thoughts, fancies, and problems, does not seek to understand the others. There is, therefore, little real communication between them. Eleanor reaches out to the others, to Theodora and to Luke; but they do not respond, except superficially. Theodora's own desire to be admired causes her to seek Luke's approval and attention. Luke seeks a mother figure but does not find one. Luke, like Arthur in *Hangsaman* and like Essex in *The Sundial*, is a charming but weak man. Several of the young men in Jackson stories are of this type, although each is a well-drawn character. Critic Warren Beck in the *Chicago Sunday Tribune* (October 18, 1959) acknowledges Miss Jackson's ability to create people but questions the plot when he says, "Some may regret the imposition of so tricky a frame upon such fine characterization." In regard to characterization, the reviewer states: "It is less the interplay between these characters which makes this novel worth reading than their relationships to the house itself, particularly that of the girl Eleanor, whose characterization is Miss Jackson's finest to date. . . ."[9] As for the book itself, the same critic felt that *The Haunting of Hill House* ranked only midway in Miss Jackson's works; it was certainly not so good as "The Lottery" but far superior to *The Sundial*.

It is true that Eleanor's characterization is one of the finest in Miss Jackson's works. It is second only to that of Merricat in the later novel *We Have Always Lived in the Castle*. There are many facets to Eleanor's personality: she can be gay, charming, and witty when she feels wanted; she is generous and willing to give of herself. At the same time, she resents Theodora's selfishness and is ready to accuse Theodora of trickery when they discover the sign on the wall. For many years Eleanor has been filled with frustration and hate: she has come to hate her mother and then finally her sister and brother-in-law for taking advantage of her more submissive and passive nature. She struggles to overcome the guilt that she feels for the death of her mother.

Although one comes to know her quite well, she remains mysterious. The mystery is a product of Eleanor's uncertainty and her mental and emotional changes, which are difficult to fathom. She is insecure and, therefore, unstable in her relationships with others and in her relationship with the house. She feels the irresistible force of the spirits and longs, finally, to submit to them. When she does decide not to leave Hill House, one must assume that she is slipping into madness.

It is interesting to note that the spirits of Hill House seem essentially evil. Through their violent behavior, they seek to terrorize the visitors into harming themselves or, at least, into leaving the premises. Their natures, apparently, correspond with those of "living" beings who also are, says Miss Jackson, basically evil. The spirits ignore Mrs. Montague's love approach as, perhaps, being naïve; but they seem to know where human weaknesses lie and which humans are most vulnerable to attack. In this case, Eleanor has been the victim.

Many reviewers appreciated Miss Jackson's power to evoke tone, mood, and especially terror. Edmund Fuller in the *New York Times Book Review* (October 18, 1959) contended that ". . . At certain moments, quietly in quick, subtle transitions of tone, Miss Jackson can summon up stark terror, make your blood chill and your scalp prickle. . . . Shirley Jackson proves again that she is the finest master currently practicing in the genre of the cryptic, haunted tale."[10]

In regard to the negative aspects of the book, Maxwell Geismar indicated in the *Saturday Revue* (October 31, 1959) that, although there are brilliant episodes in the book, the story begins and develops slowly, so that it is half over before one is captured by it. Mr. Geismar also found Miss Jackson weak in depicting the relationship between Eleanor and Theodora. He stated that the two women "engage in a curious kind of infantile Lesbian affection that is meant to be sophisticated, but is usually embarrassing."

Although many readers would not agree with Mr. Geismar about either of these points, they too find themselves as disappointed as Geismar in not receiving a rationale of the supernatural at the end of the book: "It is only when the monster at Hill House strikes at last (and how) that Miss Jackson's pen becomes charmed, or rather demonic, and the supernatural activity is really chilling. . . . After the crime tales of a William Roughead or the mystery tales of Henry James himself, we are bound to expect a 'rationale' of even the supernatural. Miss Jackson never deigns to offer this to us."[11] Since one does not receive explanations for the unusual events in Miss Jackson's stories, the reader who likes a tale tied up in a neat package will not appreciate the ambiguity in her works. Ambiguity, however, need not be considered a flaw. The resolutions of such famous stories as Edgar Allan Poe's "Ligeia" and Henry James's *The Turn of the Screw* do not provide logical explanations, nor are the stories damaged as a result.

Although Miss Jackson calls her novel a simple ghost story, *The Haunting of Hill House* is more than that. It is a novel of excellent characterization with lighthearted, witty dialogue; a combination of humor with a tragic undertone; and another glimpse of the evil that is present everywhere, even in the spirit world.

III   We Have Always Lived in the Castle

According to a letter to her mother, Shirley Jackson finished *We Have Always Lived in the Castle* on Friday, April 20, 1962, after three years of work. She had spent more time on this book than on any other, but she had been seriously ill in the meantime with bouts of asthma, colitis, arthritis in the ends of her fingers, and attacks of anxiety. But, despite the handicaps, she continued working on the book, which is, many believe, her best novel. Seldom pleased with her work and regarding this book with a degree of cynicism, she said: "I do not think this book will go far. It's short for one thing, and Stanley and the publisher and the agent all agree that it is the best writing I have ever done, which is, of course, the kiss of death on *any* book."[12] She was wrong, for *Castle* was nominated for the National Book Award, received glowing reviews, and also became a best seller.

The memorable house in this novel is the Blackwood home, one of the largest and finest houses in the area of, one supposes, New England. As in most of the stories, the setting is purposely vague, for actual place-names are never given. The lack of specific location does, in fact, emphasize the concept of the little world in isolation. This house, like the Halloran mansion and Hill House, exists at some distance apart from a small village and is the subject of much gossip. As in the two previous novels, most of the action takes place within the house or on the spacious grounds around it. The townspeople envy the Blackwoods for their money and for the fine old house, but the envy turns to fear when suddenly four persons in the household die of arsenic poisoning. The survivors of the tragedy, besides Uncle Julian who has been made an invalid, are twelve-year-old Mary Katherine (Merricat), who, it turns out, *is* the murderess, and her twenty-two-year-old sister Constance, who was tried and acquitted of the crime through lack of evidence.

Now, six years later, as the novel begins, the three have been living as recluses, hidden in the house; and the only one ever to leave the premises is Merricat, who ventures to town on Tuesdays and Fridays for groceries and for books from the library. Meanwhile, the townspeople become more and more incensed at and suspicious of the house and its inhabitants so that, when the house catches fire, the villagers feel compelled to put out the blaze but then give vent to their feelings by rushing in and smashing windows, furniture, china, everything they can find. The house, of course, is never the same. When the growing vines hide the scars (the roof is never repaired), it is no longer recognizable as the fine home it once was; and it assumes, according to Merricat, the look of a castle. By the end of the novel, the house has become a refuge for Constance and Merricat, who have vowed never to leave it. Consequently, they board up the windows, bolt the doors, clear the rubbish out of two of the rooms where they intend to remain undisturbed forever. They are now completely isolated. It is as if, in Merricat's eyes, they were living on the moon.

Miss Jackson has provided less painstaking detail of the exterior of the Blackwood house than she has given in the descriptions of the Halloran mansion and Hill House; but she does spend time on the interior as it was, six years before, when the bulk of the family were still *living*, details especially of the mother's drawing room with the thirteen-foot, light-blue silk draperies, the Dresden figurines, the rose-colored chairs. The description of the wreckage after the fire, then, is especially effective in arousing reader sympathy for the two girls and their sad plight. There is very little left in the house that is usable.

Miss Jackson has chosen to tell her story through Merricat's eyes, the first-person point of view. Since Merricat has unconventional views and suffers from sociopathic personality disturbances, the story is unusual. The first paragraph hints at the intelligence and yet the childlike strangeness of this young girl: "My name is Mary Katherine Blackwood. I am eighteen years old, and I live with my sister Constance. I have often thought that with any luck at all I could have been born a werewolf, because the two middle fingers on both my hands are the same length, but I have had to be content with what I had. I dislike washing myself, and dogs, and noise. I like my sister Constance, and Richard Plantagenet and *Amanita phalloides*, the death-cup mushroom. Everyone else in my family is dead."[13]

From this passage, one sees immediately her preoccupation with the supernatural and her interest in death. Constance, the ominous Richard III (known erroneously as a murderer), and the poisonous mushroom seem to share equal billing in her affections; yet this is not true, since her love for Constance is and always has been the strongest force in her life. In fact, her greatest fear is that Constance may one day leave her. The fact that Merricat is familiar with

Richard Plantagenet and the scientific name of the mushroom is an indication of her wide reading and her singular cleverness. At the same time, she displays her childishness in admitting that she does not like to wash. Her dislike of dogs, perhaps, is the result of being chased by them and their young owners in the village.

Merricat's thoughts come helter-skelter, often with little differentiation as to their actual importance; but, being impulsive and ruled by her emotions, she has acquired her own twisted set of values — she is so confused about right and wrong that she has, in fact, no moral sense at all. She wants to be nice to Uncle Julian because she feels sorry for him, but she never expresses remorse or sorrow for the death of the members of her family. She does not speak of the event, and one assumes from her attitude that they deserved to die. She hated them for not loving her: she was the one always sent to bed without supper while her younger brother received the love and attention she craved. On that fateful evening, Constance, disliking blackberries, was the only person who did not taste the arsenic-filled sugar. And, although Merricat was in her bedroom at the time, she knew that Constance was safe and that her despised little brother would take the most sugar.

Merricat is, undoubtedly, Miss Jackson's finest character. She is human and, despite her great crime, sympathetic and likable. Though in one sense horrifying, she is believable, capable of both intense love and intense hate. She is honest in her own innocent, twisted way; but she can scheme for what she wants. She is seemingly intelligent and yet totally mad. Because she does not trust people, she relies wholly on magic objects she hopes will ward off evil. What she does, she regards as necessary for survival. Furthermore, she has spirit; and Miss Jackson has drawn her in an originally fey manner with warmth and humor. Merricat's beliefs and actions are often funny despite their grotesqueness.

When Merricat goes to the village, she thinks of her movements as part of a game always full of dangers such as: "I lose one turn," "go back four spaces," etc. (depending upon the reactions of the villagers); and not until she reaches the black rock on the Blackwood property does she win. The actual dangers are meeting people on the street or in the store. Not only does she hate the people, being thoroughly convinced that they, in turn, hate her and all the other Blackwoods, but she wishes them dead. In her daydreams, she sees their writhing, agonized bodies lying on the streets as she steps over them; and such imaginings make her smile. Sometimes, on her way

home, the bravest of the children mock her and sing the little rhyme
made popular during the murder trial and learned, no doubt, from
their parents:

> Merricat, said Connie, would you like a cup of tea?
> Oh no, said Merricat, you'll poison me.
> Merricat, said Connie, would you like to go to sleep?
> Down in the boneyard ten feet deep! (22 - 23)

To ward off evils, she has a habit of nailing objects to a tree,
perhaps a book, a watch chain, or a scarf. She also buries objects —
her blue marbles, or a doll, or the bag of silver dollars — to achieve
her desire or to act as powerful antidotes to evil. To her, every event
is an omen of either good or bad luck; and, when she is displeased or
upset, she runs into the woods with her cat Jonas to hide in her
shelter of branches and leaves. She and Jonas have a special
relationship, and Miss Jackson depicts this relationship between
Jonas and Merricat with wit and charm. The ability to make animals
warm and human, giving them childlike qualities, is one of the ingredients of her "magic." In Miss Jackson's thinking, the fictional
character who loves animals contains more good than bad. Despite
his negative qualities, he has a benevolent heart.

Merricat and Jonas communicate easily. On this particular day she
relates: "The trees around overhead were so thick that it was always
dry inside and on Sunday morning I lay there with Jonas, listening to
his stories. All cat stories start with the statement: 'My mother, who
was the first cat, told me this,' and I lay with my head close to Jonas
and listened. There was no change coming, I thought here, only
spring; I was wrong to be so frightened." (76). Merricat knows in-
stinctively that some big change is coming that can only be evil. The
arrival of her cousin Charles Blackwood constitutes the change, for
she considers him to be an intruder and a threat to her relationship
with Constance.

Charles, one discovers, is interested only in the money Constance
keeps in the safe. He is horrified to discover that Connie, Merricat,
and Uncle Julian do not think in terms of dollars, are not concerned
with material goods; and he complains bitterly to Constance that
something should be done about Merricat, when he finds the bag of
silver dollars she has buried and the gold watch chain she has nailed
to the tree. From Merricat's standpoint, his first offense is the usur-
pation of their father's room and belongings. When he threatens

Merricat, she knows that she must resort to powerful agents to encourage him to leave; and she breaks his bedroom mirror. Later, she removes most of the movable properties from his room, fills the bed with grass and sticks, and pours water over the mattress in the belief that he may not recognize his room and so leave it. Needless to say, Charles is furious. There is much humor in Merricat's unusual escapades, although they are serious to her.

Charles is another of the unsympathetic, weak young males found so often in Miss Jackson's stories and novels. He, like Essex and Arthur Langdon, is selfish and self-indulgent; but of them all, Charles is the most mercenary, the most ruthless. He has, in fact, very few good qualities, but then the reader sees him only through Merricat's eyes. She knows that she has cause to fear and hate him. The greatest fear lies in Charles's influence over the lovely, gentle Constance. If her sister decides to leave the house forever, Merricat knows that she may be sent away. As it happens, the last day of their comfortable existence comes when Merricat brushes Charles's lighted pipe off the dresser into the wastebasket and causes a fire. Charles runs to the village for help; but, by the time the fire engines arrive, the blaze has control of most of the upper part of the house.

During the excitement Charles's only concern has been with the impossible task of removing the safe from the house. Meanwhile, a frightened Constance and Merricat hide on the porch behind the vines and watch the firemen subdue the flames. Then when the blaze is out, chief fireman Jim Donell, one of the villagers whom Merricat hates, saunters back to the truck, stoops suddenly, picks up a rock, and throws it through a window. The villagers, long envious and fearful of the Blackwoods, gleefully follow suit, smashing and destroying. Realizing their danger, Merricat and Constance attempt to run toward the woods, but the crowd encircles and taunts them.

Finally, with roles reversed and with Merricat taking care of Constance, who runs with an apron over her face so that the crowd cannot see her, they reach Merricat's secret hiding place. The destruction is halted only when the doctor arrives announcing Uncle Julian's death of a heart attack. The crowd disperses; and, from their safe nook, Merricat and Constance hear the ambulance come in the middle of the night to take Uncle Julian away. At this point in the story, Merricat, thinking of the villagers, vows that she is going to put death in their food. When Constance asks, "The way you did before?" Merricat answers, "Yes, . . . the way I did before." Supposedly Constance has not spoken of Merricat's crime in six years;

and, although the reader may have suspected the truth, this indication is the first that he has had of Merricat's guilt and of her sister's
loyalty. By withholding Merricat's secret, Miss Jackson has built the
suspense and made her revelation the climax of the novel.

Merricat has always wished herself on the moon, that magic land
where, she believes, all her dreams will come true and where she can
escape when the present environment becomes too ugly. The morning after the fire as they awaken under the trees, she knows instinc-
tively that Constance will never leave her and that she need fear no
longer. "We are on the moon at last," she tells Constance. One
never knows what Constance is thinking, but she has regressed in her
desire to be with people, for now she wants only to hide. The horrors
of the night have convinced her that she and Merricat must shut
themselves up and never see anyone. As to Charles, he has dis-
appeared, apparently, when he could not remove the safe.

When the girls finally return to the house, they are dismayed at
the almost total destruction; only the kitchen and Uncle Julian's
room are usable. The fire has destroyed a large part of the roof, a
feature that pleases Merricat; for now it is, in her eyes, "a castle
turreted and open to the sky." After helping Constance clean the
kitchen and prepare a room for sleeping, Merricat puts cardboard
over the windows so that no one will be able to look in. The only
light comes from the open door, which they will allow to stand ajar
as long as no intruder is near. Now the reader sees how withdrawn
the girls have become: they are willing to sacrifice light for privacy.
Thereafter, the villagers appear singly and quietly, sometimes at
night, to leave a note with a basket of food to indicate that they are
sorry. Despite hardships, the two girls consider themselves contented
and happy; in fact, throughout the story, except for tense moments,
the atmosphere is peaceful, even cheerful — certainly not depressing
or gloomy.

Because events and persons are seen through Merricat's eyes,
neither Constance nor Uncle Julian is a fully developed character.
Uncle Julian's illness, caused by the arsenic poisoning, keeps him in
a wheelchair; and his one preoccupation is the gathering of material
for a book about the day that the family died. Through his
reminiscenses and Merricat's memories, the reader sees that neither
the father nor the mother of the Blackwood family was an admirable
character; but lack of sympathy for the family is necessary, of course,
for the reader to empathize with Merricat and Constance. Uncle
Julian is very like Richard Halloran of *The Sundial:* besides being an

invalid, he has lapses of memory, is often peevish, and requires close attention, which, in Uncle Julian's case, he receives from Constance. He is very fond of his niece and refuses to believe her guilty.

Constance is consistently thoughtful, kind, loving, and desperately loyal to her younger sister. Perhaps because Merricat has always been a bit abnormal, and thus the black sheep of the family and the target of abuse, Constance has taken care of her and protected her. When Merricat was sent to bed without supper, Constance quietly brought her a tray. It is she who does the cooking and who was doing the cooking on the day of the murders. This, in addition to the fact that she washed out the sugar bowl before the doctor came (she said there was a spider in it), pointed to her guilt.

Understanding Merricat's crime, Constance has allowed herself to appear guilty to avoid, one assumes, her sister's being confined in a mental institution; but, in doing so, she has doomed herself. She has always been shy; but after the fire, one suspects that she too, has become paranoid, perhaps never to recover. In the past, she has been the protector; but, after the fire, Merricat is the dominant personality, the protector. Merricat has now what she has always wanted: the assurance that she and Constance will remain together with no one else to compete for Constance's attention. This state of happiness and seclusion from outside interference are the equivalent of "being on the moon." Having no moral sense, she will not be tortured by guilt for anything she has done, nor will she understand the sacrifices Constance has made for her.

Max Steele in his *New York Herald Tribune* review praises Miss Jackson's imaginative handling of Merricat when he observes that

Shirley Jackson looks at the world as practically nobody else does and describes it in a way almost everybody would like to emulate. Her story has so much suspense a reader may not see at first how beautifully she has avoided the textbook case-history in showing us the fascinating workings of Mary Katherine Blackwood's surprising mind. In fact, when one does realize how much Miss Jackson knows about people and how light yet probing her touch can be, it is then that one wonders if it is not time for her to forget "The Lottery" and to let her characters take over a story of their own in a much bigger book. In the meantime we can be happy that we have seen Mary Katherine Blackwood and been allowed into the Castle where she lives.[14]

Again, as in Miss Jackson's other novels, even the minor characters have definite personalities: Mrs. Clarke is a loyal friend who tries to rescue Constance from a dismal future but fails. Mrs. Wright, who comes to tea once with Mrs. Clarke, is a timid soul who is humorous in her inability to resist asking questions about the mass murder but is then too frightened to drink her own tea or eat the sandwich beside it. Jim Donell, the fire chief, enjoys baiting Merricat when he meets her in town; he has a vicious streak that shows itself when he signals the destruction of the house after the fire. And Charles, a major-minor character, is superficially charming but treacherous and greedy; and he finds he is no match for Merricat. The mother of the Blackwood family, although not present in the novel, is spoken of as a selfish, domineering woman who was so fond of her beautiful drawing room that she would not allow her children to enter it. The father also had a strong will, a condition that resulted in many family quarrels. He was parsimonious, and according to his brother, Uncle Julian, not overly honest. Mr. Blackwood and the domineering Mr. Halloran of *The Sundial* would, no doubt, have had much in common. Of the characters even Jonas, the cat, has a definite personality, for he, in Merricat's eyes, is and behaves like a human.

All of the characters are authentic; and Merricat, with the mental quirks that mark her as abnormal, is believable and real. One not only empathizes with her but likes and pities her. Though now eighteen years old, she is a lost child who becomes crafty through the necessity of survival; and she will always remain a child. It is interesting to speculate as to the future of Constance and Merricat, alone in the house. How long can they, or anyone, survive without the assistance of the community?

Again, the evil prevalent in man is shown by the actions of the members of the community, individually and collectively — in the mob. Yet, there is a note of hope, for to salve their guilty consciences, certain persons do come forward to offer help by way of food, but how long will this continue? How long does it take to ease a ruffled conscience?

The deceased members of the Blackwood family, too, have their share of guilt; and amoral Merricat, who maneuvers in her own way and for her own benefit, might well be evil personified, except that the reader cannot accept her as such. The only really good, blameless individual of the group is Constance; and perhaps she also might be less than perfect if one knew her better, for one feels that these are genuine people — not characters for the moment. An important lesson may be that the truly noble people often place themselves at the mercy of other less noble souls, thereby bringing about their own destruction. On the other hand, there is nothing sentimental in the handling of Constance, for at the end of the book Merricat says, "I wonder if I *could* eat a child if I had the chance," and Constance says rather matter of factly, "I doubt if I could cook one"; but she has said earlier, in regard to Charles, "The least Charles could have done was shoot himself through the head in the driveway."

Reviewers of *We Have Always Lived in the Castle* agree that Miss Jackson writes with strength and imagination; that she presents a well-laid and well-kept plot; that her characterizations are superb; and that the charm and comedy of the book are stronger than the horror in it. As the *Time* critic says: "The book manages the ironic miracle of convincing the reader that a house inhabited by a lunatic, a poisoner and a pyromaniac is a world more rich in sympathy, love and subtlety than the real world outside."[15]

But the elusiveness of Miss Jackson's isolated worlds often makes critical appraisal difficult. The reader is pleased with what he has experienced, but analysis of that experience is not always successful. Along these lines, Ihab Hassan *(New York Times Book Review)* states:

I have always felt that some writers should be read and never reviewed. Their talent is haunting and utterly oblique. Their mastery of craft seems complete. Even before reading Shirley Jackson's latest novel, I would have thought her case to be clear; she is of that company. And now Miss Jackson has made it even more difficult for a reviewer to seem pertinent; all he can do is bestow praise. Yet praise can take many forms. Perhaps the best thing one can say of this author is that she offers an alternative to the canonical view of "seriousness" in literature. Like the late Isak Dinesen, she is a meticulous story teller who can evoke the reality of the times without invoking its current, cloying cliches. Her work moves on the invisible shadow line between fantasy and verisimilitude: it also hovers between innocence and dark knowledge. Above all, her work never averts itself from the human thing, which it quickens with chilly laughter or fabulous imaginings.[16]

Louis Untermeyer, another of Miss Jackson's admirers, emphasizes her unusual accomplishments in this novel: "It is unquestionably Shirley Jackson's best book. It is also one of the most beautiful books I have read in years. It achieves the incredible: an unbelievable combination of terror and tenderness, of horror and pity. Eerie though the situation is, and strange though the characters may be, no reader can fail to participate in the events and be moved by them. . . . She has planned, put together and performed pure magic."[17] The true magic of Shirley Jackson has nothing to do with witchcraft or with mysterious occurrences of the occult; her magic results from the original manner with which she presents an unconventional story and with the unique but authentic people she creates. To these elements she adds wit and humor. Despite the grotesque touches and the tragic undertones of its finish, the novel has a happy ending — if by *happy* one means that the main characters are contented with their situation as it is. The reader rejoices in the happiness of their illusory world but is too much a citizen of the real world not to be aware of the dangers ahead. Still, he accepts Shirley Jackson's world on her terms and is willing to suspend disbelief.

Although the novel was successful, the play was not; it closed three nights after it opened on Broadway at the Barrymore Theater. In the conclusion of a review in *Commonweal* (November 11, 1966), Wilfrid Sheed had this to say about the stage version of *Castle:* "To be fair, it might be added that Shirley Jackson's special note of offhand malignancy would probably be hard to translate to the stage, even if you were trying."[18] In the play, Merricat apparently becomes an unreal witchlike character who communicates with the dead. Miss Jackson undoubtedly would not have approved. The real Merricat is closer to the Lizzie Borden image, a subject whom Miss Jackson studied with interest and whose influence can be seen in both *The Sundial* (in the local acquitted murderess) and in *We Have Always Lived in the Castle.* As to the house, Merricat's castle endures and remains an influence in its environment, as did Hill House and the Halloran mansion.

CHAPTER 6

The Family Chronicles

I Life Among the Savages

ALTHOUGH *Life Among the Savages* was published in 1953 (between *Hangsaman* and *The Bird's Nest*), most of the anecdotes included in it had been published previously as short stories. For instance, "Charles," the tale of Laurie's kindergarten experience, had appeared in the July, 1948, issue of *Mademoiselle;* "My Son and the Bully," in the October, 1949, issue of *Good Housekeeping.* In *Harper's* were "The Third Baby Is the Easiest," "First Car Is the Hardest," "The Night We All Had Grippe." Other stories included are "List Found in a Coat Pocket" from *Vogue;* and "The Box," "Monday Morning," "Shopping Trip," and "Visions of Sugar Plums" were first published in *Woman's Home Companion.* All of these stories belong together since they are humorous accounts, although exaggerated, of events in the Hyman household. Miss Jackson has arranged them chronologically and has added description and related events to give a more complete family picture. Officially (in library listings), both *Life Among the Savages* and the later *Raising Demons* are classified as nonfiction.

The book, written in first person by Miss Jackson, begins *in medias res* in Vermont and then flashes back to the leaving of the New York apartment and to the search for a suitable home in Vermont. The first paragraph establishes the tone and displays the comfortable, easy wit that prevails throughout Miss Jackson's autobiographical works:

Our house is old, and noisy, and full. When we moved into it we had two children and about five thousand books; I expect that when we finally overflow and move out again we will have perhaps twenty children and easily half a million books; we also own assorted beds and tables and rocking horses and lamps and doll dresses and ship models and paint brushes and literally thousands of socks. This is the way of life my husband and I have fallen into, inadvertently, as though we had fallen into a well and decided that since there was no way out we might as well stay there and set up a chair and a desk and a light of some kind; even though this *is* our way of life, and the only one we know, it is occasionally bewildering, and perhaps even inexplicable to the sort of person who does not have that swift, accurate conviction that he is going to step on a broken celluloid doll in the dark. I cannot think of a preferable way of life, except one without children and without books, going on soundlessly in an apartment hotel where they do the cleaning for you and send up your meals and all you have to do is lie on a couch and — as I say, I cannot think of a preferable way of life, but then I have had to make a good many compromises, all told.[1]

The chosen house ("the former Fielding house") — and one can see why the Hymans were impressed with it — is the oldest in the neighborhood and perhaps the third oldest in the township. It was built around 1820, she states, as a manor house in the center of a large farm. Modeled after a Greek temple, it has "four massive white pillars across the front." Impressive as the house is, it soon becomes simply a backdrop for family activity and is eclipsed by the colorful individuals who have taken possession.

The two Hyman children who move in with their parents are Laurie (Laurence) and Jannie (Joanne). Within the next six years, Sally (Sarah) is the next to appear; and last of all comes Barry. Because he is the oldest, Laurie is the central figure in most of the stories dealing with the children; and he is approximately nine years old when the book ends.

One of the first and the most famous of the anecdotes is the incident of "Charles." As Miss Jackson tells it, during Laurie's first few weeks in kindergarten, he came home every day to report the misdeeds of Charles, a little boy who caused little girls to say naughty words, who threw chalk, yelled in school, and not only kicked the gymnasium teacher, but also hit his own teacher. The family, duly impressed with the audaciousness of this Charles, was eager for Mrs. Hyman (Shirley Jackson) to meet his mother on Parent-Teachers' Association night. At the meeting, Mrs. Hyman searched the assembly for the suitably worn, frazzled-looking woman who would be the mother of such a boy. Having no success, she chatted instead with the teacher who mentioned that Laurie had had trouble adjusting to school, but now, with a few lapses, he has been doing well. In answer to Mrs. Hyman's question about Charles, the teacher looked puzzled. "Charles?. . . We don't have any Charles in the kindergarten."

The surprise ending with Laurie's being the culprit is more effective for reader interest than the actual situation; for there really was a cantankerous little boy named Charles who caused the teacher and the school authorities much grief and much hand wringing. This is the type of manipulation of fact that Miss Jackson uses; and, while it may deny a minor truth, it nevertheless makes a more entertaining story.

One of the funniest events is the cat-bat-airgun episode. Mr. Hyman (Miss Jackson refers to him always as "my husband") has bought an airgun to shoot the rat that he suspects lurks in the cellar. In reference to the gun, she says: "I have never really believed that my husband is the Kit Carson type, but it is remotely possible that occasionally a feeling for the life romantic overcomes him; this airgun was large and menacing and he told me, in that terribly responsible voice men get to using when they are telling their wives about machinery, or guns, or politics, that he got it for target practice" (403).

The primary target was to be the rat, but somehow, probably because of the noise of the spectators, the rat chose to remain hidden; not long after, Ninki, the female-cat-hunter, brought into the kitchen to her own dish the chipmunk she had captured. The chipmunk, very much alive, eluded the cat and raced for a tall plant on the windowsill.

Part of the humor lies in Miss Jackson's knack for endowing animals with almost human qualities: ". . . Ninki, in a sort of frenzy, hurried into the dining room where my husband was just finishing his coffee and talked him into going into the kitchen to see her chipmunk in the plant. My husband took one look and went for his airgun" (404).

Mr. Hyman had trouble getting "a bead" on the chipmunk, mostly because the cat was in the way. When Mrs. Hyman came to see, she suggested putting a paper bag over the animal. She describes the action as follows:

Ninki was by this time irritated beyond belief by the general air of incompetence exhibited in the kitchen, and she went into the living room and got Shax, who is extraordinarily lazy and never catches his own chipmunks, but who is, at least, a cat, and preferable, Ninki saw clearly, to a man with a gun. Shax sized up the situation with a cynical eye, gave my husband and his gun the coldest look I have ever seen a cat permit himself, and then leaped onto the window sill and sat on the other side of the flowerpot (404).

With a cat sitting on each side of the plant, the chipmunk began nervously to sway from one side to the other; and each cat batted him as he came close. In the excitement, Mr. Hyman shot the airgun without really meaning to, missed the cats and the chipmunk, but broke the window; and through it the chipmunk thoughtfully made a hurried exit.

A similar incident occurred one evening not long after when a triumphant Ninki again ushered in a victim. Mrs. Hyman, lying on the couch reading a mystery story, had just begged her husband to make the cat take it outside. This time Ninki's supper, a "full-grown and horribly active bat," made a grand sweep of the living room while Mrs. Hyman shrieked and hid under the blanket. Again Mr. Hyman called for his gun. Mrs. Hyman — still under the blanket — was aware of stealthy movement within the room, with her husband tiptoeing and the cat apparently behind him, for he was saying, "Don't *hurry,* for heaven's sake, give me a chance to *aim.*" The thought occurred to her that the bat might be on her; for Mr. Hyman, in a reassuring manner, told her to hold perfectly still:

"Is it on the *blanket?*" I insisted hysterically, "on me?"
"Listen," my husband said crossly, "if you keep on shaking like that, I'll *never* be able to hit it. Hold still, and I'm sure to miss you." . . . I do not know what the official world's record might be for getting out from under a blanket, flying across a room, opening a door and a screen door, and getting outside onto a porch with both doors closed behind you, but if it is more than about four seconds I broke it. I thought the bat was chasing me, for one thing. And I knew that, if the bat was chasing me, my husband was aiming that gun at it, wherever it was. (406)

The sequence of events here testifies to Miss Jackson's narrative skill, her knack for clever dialogue and, all in all, her good storytelling technique. The next paragraph is a further example:

Inside, there was a series of crashes. I recognized the first as the report of the airgun. The second sounded irresistibly like a lamp going over, which is what it turned out to be. The third I could not identify from the porch, but my husband said later that it was Ninki trying to get out of the way of the airgun and knocking over the andirons. Then my husband spoke angrily to

Ninki, and Ninki snarled. Each of them, it seemed, thought the other one had frightened the bat, which had left the blanket when I did, although not half so fast, and was now circling gaily around the chandelier. (406 - 07)

Later, after a long silence, she asked if he were all right and if it were safe to come in. "I don't know," he replied, looking at her bitterly, "have you got a ticket?" Shortly after this fiasco, the airgun found its way to the top shelf of the pantry, where, apparently, it remained until the family moved.

Of the stories included in this book, Mr. Hyman's favorite was "The Night We All Had Grippe," which he considered to be as funny as anything written by Thurber. In this account, during the course of an evening, after Mrs. Hyman had bedded her sick family in the various rooms, dispensed aspirin and the habitual glasses of apple juice, and gotten smoking equipment for her husband and brandy for herself, there began what amounted to a game of musical beds, which involved at irregular intervals changes of personnel — including the dog who slept on the bottom bunk of Laurie's two-decker bed — and of pillows and blankets.

At the end of the long hectic night, there was a confusion of bedding, supplies, and people — and also the mystery of a missing blanket. In Miss Jackson's words, "The puzzle is, of course, what became of the blanket from Sally's bed? I took it off her crib and put it on the bottom half of the double-decker, but the dog did not have it when he woke up, and neither did any of the other beds. It was a blue-patterned patchwork quilt, and has not been seen since, and I would most particularly like to know where it got to. As I say, we are very short of blankets" (471).

At the end of the book, Mrs. Hyman brings home the newest addition to the family, Barry, to whom the children refer as "it." Laurie asks, "Is *that* it you're carrying . . . that *little* thing?" and later he says, "It's pretty small . . . is that the best you could get?" Mrs. Hyman answers with irritation, "I tried to get another, a bigger one, . . . but the doctor said this was the only one left." Finally nine-year-old Laurie, feeling called upon to make some congratulatory remark, says, "I guess it *will* be nice for you, though . . . something to keep you busy now we're all grown up"(528).

The most frequent source of humor is allied with Miss Jackson's insight into the everyday nuances and workings of the average family. She understands the role of the mother and the helplessness mothers feel in the unexpected behavior of their offspring and in the overwhelming work load they encounter. She also understands children and has a true ear for their speech. The Hyman family was far from average, what with two brilliant writer-parents and four talented, precocious children; nevertheless, there are experiences such as additions to the family, shopping trips to the city, bicycle accidents, buying a first car, coping with first-grade teachers, borrowing money from the bank — experiences that are central to most middle-class families in which the mother finds herself cast as maid, cook, manager of accounts, chauffeur, referee, and nurse — all with smiling patience.

II Raising Demons

Four years after *Life Among the Savages* had made its popular debut with the humorous accounts of the Hyman family, Shirley Jackson presented its sequel, *Raising Demons* (1957). As so often happens, the second book did not achieve the popularity of the first; whatever the reason, Miss Jackson attributed its poorer reception to inadequate publicity. Many of the episodes in this work also had been published earlier in magazines: "The Sneaker Crisis," "Worldly Goods," "The Clothespin Dolls," and "Lucky to Get Away" had appeared in *Woman's Day*; "An International Incident," in *The New Yorker*; "It's Only a Game" and "Aunt Gertrude," in *Harper's Magazine*; "Family Magician," "So Late on Sunday Morning," "Don't Tell Daddy," and "Every Boy Should Learn to Play the Trumpet," in *Woman's Home Companion*, and so on. The Hymans did not take the stories seriously, and Miss Jackson, although appreciative of their salability, considered them "potboilers." No one, however, after reading these anecdotes can discount her talents as a humorist. Like Mark Twain, she could make accounts of ordinary events appear hilarious.

At the beginning of the book the family, prompted by a shortage of space, neighborhood enthusiasm, and commercial enterprise, has decided to move into a larger house within the town. The packing process with the placing of the goods in storage is not only a major operation but a source of humor; and the storage list with its odd symbols (B.O. for Bad Order, M.E. for Moth-Eaten, S & M for Scratched and Marred) supplies them with amusement during their temporary stay in the house of friends who live seventy miles away. Miss Jackson recalls:

Gradually, during the long summer days, our list became as intimate a part of our daily life as the washing machine grumbling to itself in the kitchen, or the deep freeze doggedly making popsicles downstairs. "Small Round Table S & M," I would cry gaily to Laurie, and he would be allowed one minute before answering, "Girls' room, corner near the window." "147, Fire Lighter," my husband would come back, and if no one could guess it (far corner of the cellar, leaning against the wall) another penny went into the pot for Mr. Cobb. D. R. Table puzzled us, until we realized that it was not a Table Dented and Rusted, but our old dining room table; Bundle Metal Discs B.O. were not a little sack of Greek coins my husband had somehow overlooked, but the metal records for our old-fashioned music box, although how Mr. Cobb was able to estimate that they were B.O. is beyond me.[2]

The "new" old house with its crooked gatepost (and she does describe accurately the house in which they lived) had been made into four apartments, which now reverted to the structure of a one-family house. Having much faith in the realtor and little experience with old houses, the Hymans find that the plumbing needs an overhauling, the furnace needs repair, the roof needs new shingles, the electrician must rip out the dining room ceiling; and all the repair men give advice about the crooked gatepost.

Expenses have a way of mounting; everyone except Dad has decided that a new car is absolutely essential, especially after Mrs. Hyman and the children have had a slight accident with the old family car, which now has "its nose smashed in with one headlight hanging crooked." Mother and Laurie have estimated that it will take approximately one month of subtle maneuvering and silent pressure to make Father change his ideas about a new car. And sure enough, just four days short of the month Father agrees that, since they are to be in debt for the rest of their lives anyway with the house payments, they might as well buy a car too and "go bankrupt in style." Consequently, to go with the shiny new brown-and-cream station wagon, Mother buys Beekman (Barry) a new car-chair equipped with a small steering wheel and gearshift lever: "By the end of a week I was no longer fumbling wildly for the brake pedal in the new car, and Beekman was manipulating his steering wheel and gearshift with such wild abandon and skillful maneuvering as to earn himself the title of Mad-Dog Beekman" (604). Barry, a unique character, receives many names. At one stage he is B. B., then Mr. B., later Mr. Beetle, and finally Mr. Beekman, which he remains until he is ready for nursery school.

For a time thereafter on shopping days, everyone goes along for the ride. On one occasion, when they barely scrape into a parking space with no room to get out on the driver's side, Laurie comments:

"Jeepers, . . . cut it a little close, didn't you?"

"It was Beekman," I said nervously. "He kept pulling to the left."

"Jeepers," Laurie said to Beekman, "you want to watch where you're going, kid." (605)

One weekend, while Barry is still Barry, Mother is to have a get-together with former college friends away from home. She makes elaborate preparations so that the older children will stay with friends and be out of Mr. Hyman's way. To be helpful, she leaves a long note, a "simple chronological outline" (a timetable of the children's activities), with directions for mealtimes, especially for Barry, including orders for the milkman, information about the supper casserole, the jar labeled "Mayonnaise" with coffee to heat up, and the disposition of Jannie's jelly beans at bedtime ("Six jellybeans is plenty"). On Sunday evening, expecting the family to be in bed ("Do not wait up for me," she has told them), Mother arrives to find the house lighted and no one in sight. A note on the coffee table reads:

SUNDAY . . . Barry and/or dog ate all directions. Have taken all children incl. Barry to hamburger stand for dinner, movies. Barry fond of movies, went yesterday too, also fr. fr. potatoes. Don't wait up for us. Casserole on kitchen table, cats not fed. Milkman left two dozen eggs. Jannie says six jellybeans is not plenty. Leave front door unlocked. Jar in refrigerator labeled Mayonnaise was mayonnaise. (588)

The humor here stems from reversal of expectation. The short laconic note indicates the new direction of events, with Mr. Hyman making his own on-the-spot arrangements. Nothing has turned out as planned.

In another example of reversal — of situation in this case — Mother comes home rather late from a ladies' poker game; and, after tiptoeing through the house to make sure that the children are properly covered, she arrives at her own dresser:

I had thought to get undressed without turning on the light, and I found my dresser, where there was supposed to be a package of matches. I found my comb and a pair of earrings and what seemed in the dark to be some small furry animal; after a gasping minute I succeeded in identifying it as one of Sally's slippers, although I could not imagine what it was doing on my dresser unless Sally had been dancing up there in front of the mirror again.

"Who's that?" said my husband suddenly in the darkness.

"It's the Good Fairy," I said. "Didn't you leave a tooth under your pillow?"

"Oh," he said. Then, after a minute, "How was the poker game?" (725)

Her answers are noncommittal; and, as to winning, she reminds him that she did not interrogate him when he came home late, all worn out. He concedes.

In most cases, Father remains on the sidelines — presumably since as a teacher-writer-critic he is at work in the den, reading and writing important articles and books, when he is not in the classroom. In one notable instance, however, the spotlight falls on Father when he is asked to be a judge in the Miss Vermont beauty contest. Laurie is horrified at the news and at what his friends will say. Mother, after the first fit of convulsive laughter, has mixed feelings about the event, especially when she finds that Mr. Hyman is to ride to Burlington with the local beauty queen. And, for the few days of the contest, until the grisly business is over, no one ventures downtown near the barber shop or the newsstand.

As the children — Laurie, Jannie (Joanne), Sally, and Barry — become older, they develop eccentricities that attest to their creativity. Sally's forte is magic; and, until ordered to stop, she goes about putting spells on people and things, such as the refrigerator. Barry, happily and trustingly, follows her into the land of make-believe with visits to the magic tree house of Sally's imaginary friend Pudge. For a time, Sally is the only one who can understand Barry's own special lingo.

Laurie, the oldest, has developed many interests, aside from the fascination with coin collecting that he and his father share; one of these interests is the desire to play the trumpet. For a time Mother resists the idea of lessons, until a seemingly unrelated incident forces her to reconsider her position. She discovers one day that the old, stubborn refrigerator, with a door that often sticks, appears to be exuding a ghastly odor. When she calls the repairman, he orders her to leave the house immediately and to get everyone else out. The leaking gas is poisonous, he says. Later two men come to haul away the offending appliance while opening windows and doors to air the house and eliminate all traces of gas.

Mother now talks Father into buying not only a new refrigerator but also a dishwasher and at the same time a new linoleum floor covering to keep the rest of the kitchen from looking shabby. Shortly thereafter, an unhappy Laurie tells his mother that he has lost the sodium bisulphite his father gave him to use in his chemistry set. He has put it in a pan with acid and has placed the pan on the kitchen radiator, but the heat must have been turned on because the pan is now dry and empty. With a sudden thought Mother asks, "Laurie . . . that sodium what-do-you-call-it and the other stuff mixed together — what would they do?" He doesn't know; that was what he was going to find out. Does she know where it is? Mother looks about her new kitchen and (in a masterpiece of understatement) suggests that he not mention it to his father yet. "Do you think he might take away my chemistry set?" he asks. When she assures him that she is certain of it, he replies, "Then can I learn to play the trumpet?" (676). With an economy of words, Miss Jackson allows the reader to guess the solution of the missing gasses at the same time that Mother does. And the trumpet lessons turn out to be a reward for silence. There are cases like this when Father is somewhat duped, yet the new kitchen is for the good of all and presumably Mother deserves it, even if they cannot afford it.

Another of Laurie's major interests and one that involved the whole town was Little League baseball. The Hymans and the villagers became enthusiastic baseball fans. All games were well attended, but the most trying moments for Mother and Father came when Laurie pitched. Much humor stems from the anxiety of the parents of the players:

"The umpire called Laurie's next pitch ball three, although it was clearly a strike, and I was yelling, 'You're blind, you're blind.' I could hear my husband shouting to throw the bum out" (684).

As in *Life Among the Savages*, the humorous, often typical, family situations with which readers can identify are the major appeal of the book. And the little touches, the personalizing of animals — the smiling mouse, tapping his fingers irritably against the drawer, and Gato the cowardly cat — add charm to the work.

CHAPTER 7

Overview

I *Principles of and for a Writer*

A MONG Miss Jackson's non-fiction works are the essays about the craft of writing. These are significant to this study in that they embody the principles around which Miss Jackson formed her own works. Each rule is one that applies to her own stories. Three of the lectures, presented earlier at college and writers' conferences, are included in the anthology *Come Along With Me*. Of these, "Experience and Fiction" later appeared in the January, 1969, issue of *The Writer*. As the title implies, all experience counts for something; the writer regards the events of his life as a potential source for stories. These events may have to be manipulated and shaped, for true experiences as such seldom make good fiction. Along with this realization, she indicates several specific truths about fiction writing: ". . . no scene and no character can be allowed to wander off by itself; there must be some furthering of the story in every sentence, and even the most fleeting background characters must partake of the story in some way; they must be characters peculiar to *this* story and no other."[1]

Miss Jackson practices what she preaches, for her background characters are individuals. Mr. and Mrs. Dudley in *The Haunting of Hill House* are good examples, for they appear as eccentric as the old house of which they are caretakers. In the short story form, following this advice is more difficult, but such characters as the housekeeper in "The Rock" and the storekeepers in "Home," "Renegade," and "The Summer People" — who are sources of important advice or information — show that Miss Jackson uses her characters to advantage. They are also appropriate to the surroundings in which she places them.

A second point Miss Jackson makes is that "people in stories are

155

called characters because that is what they are. They are not real
people. Therefore the writer should not try to transfer real people
literally to his pages of fiction. He does not need pages and pages of
description. A person in a story is identified through small things —
little gestures, turns of speech, automatic reactions. . . ." (209). In
the same way, Mrs. Dudley is remembered for her automatic
responses to the visitors at Hill House. It should be noted that, even
in the autobiographical family tales, the characters and events are
heightened and shaped to conform to Miss Jackson's purposes.

Thereafter, Miss Jackson gives several instances of experiences she
used in the process of creating stories. One of these is her account of
how she happened to write *The Haunting of Hill House;* another is
the family interview with the income-tax man, which she turned into
a short story; and another involved the night that all of the family,
including herself, became ill with the grippe, one of her funniest
stories. This particular lecture ends with her acknowledgment of a
letter from a lady in Indiana who wanted to earn some extra money.
The lady, who asked where Miss Jackson got her ideas for stories and
stated that she, herself, could "never make up anything good," had
apparently never considered shaping her own experiences.

Another of Miss Jackson's favorite lectures is entitled "Biography
of a Story," and it was given in conjunction with a reading of "The
Lottery." She presents a history of the famous short story and then a
detailed account of the public reactions to it, including excerpts of
letters from all over the world. The third of the lectures included in
the anthology, "Notes for a Young Writer," was originally intended
as a stimulus for her daughter Sally; but she again cites principles exhibited in her own works. Among the "do's" and "don't's" she
warns: the reader will willingly suspend disbelief for a time, but he
will not suspend reason: a story is an uneasy bargain with the reader.
The author's objective is to play fair and to keep the reader interested — his role is to keep reading. The writer has the right to
assume that the reader will accept the story on the author's terms,
but the story must have a surface tension that can be stretched but
not shattered.

The story should move as naturally and easily as possible without
any unnecessary side trips. The writer must *always* make the duller
parts of his story work for him: "the necessary passage of time, the
necessary movement must not stop the story dead, but must push it
forward" (245). The writer must describe only what is necessary; his
"coloring words, particularly adjectives and adverbs, must be used

where they will do the most good." As has been observed previously, she, herself, uses adjectives sparingly and makes excellent use of strong nouns and verbs.) "Inanimate objects," she states, "are best described in use or motion" (246). The writer must use a great deal of economy in written speech, and he must spend time listening to people talking, noting the patterns of speech reflected in the speaking. A writer's characters must be consistent — in speech and action. Also, the would-be writer must remember that he is living in a world of people, and he must think in terms of concrete rather than abstract nouns.

He must realize that the beginning and ending of a story belong together and that the ending is implicit in the beginning. For instance, the first line of "The Beautiful Stranger," which reads: "What might be called the first intimation of strangeness occurred at the railroad station," foreshadows the ending in which Margaret has lost all sense of reality and no longer knows where she is. But even "The Lottery," which begins with a pleasant summer day, shows traces of tension within a few lines; and the reader (looking back) can see that the ending, surprise though it may be, has been adequately planned from the beginning.

A portrait artist selects his materials carefully; he mixes here, blends there, and focuses always on the evolving subject on his canvas; and what he chooses to include in his scheme tells much about him as an individual. In the same way, Miss Jackson has chosen to include the specific subjects that are the most meaningful to her as an artist, and her themes and the characters of her special world represent evil cloaked in seeming good; prejudice and hypocrisy; the character whose mind escapes the bounds of reality; the suspense and terror of the helpless protagonist-victim; and loneliness and frustration.

II *Characteristics*

The subjects she has *ignored* in presenting her material, however, may also be significant in revealing the characteristics of her work. For example, the major characters in her stories are rarely elderly; they tend to be young, often teen-agers or persons in early middle age. In *Road Through the Wall*, the focus is on the fourteen-and fifteen-year-olds of Pepper Street; in *Hangsaman*, the schizoid Natalie is seventeen and just entering college; in *The Bird's Nest*, the multiple personality of Elizabeth is in her early twenties; in *The Haunting of Hill House*, the psychic researchers are in their late twenties and early thirties; in *The Sundial*, although Mrs. Halloran is a main character, the younger persons in the household receive equal emphasis — Gloria, Maryjane, Julia, Arabella, and the ten-year-old Fancy who is to become Mrs. Halloran's heir; in *We Have Always Lived in the Castle*, Merricat is eighteen and Constance is twenty-eight. In the short stories, also, except for those cases of kind, harmless-looking grandmothers with benevolent exteriors and warped interiors, most of the protagonists are "youngish."

One sees these people most often in isolation; and, aside from the instances of social interaction that reveal prejudice, one observes them in their loneliness. They are single people; and discounting the brief glimpse into the unhappy married state of the families of *Road Through the Wall*, Miss Jackson does not deal with marital relationships. Her heroines are unmarried; and, while the early-"thirtyish" ladies in her stories may suffer from sexual frustrations (about which nothing is said), no one in all of the stories has a love affair. One finds in them no love scenes and no sexual deviates; in fact, Miss Jackson avoids sex altogether.

The characters are often concerned, instead, with establishing their own identity. The teen-agers on Pepper Street in *Road Through the Wall* are vying for attention and recognition, and rivalry also exists among the families — the Robertses, the Martins, and the Donalds — because each wants to be important in the eyes of the community. In *Hangsaman*, Natalie struggles with her in-securities; she wants to be appreciated for what she is, but the resul-tant Tony-Natalie conflict almost destroys her. In *The Bird's Nest*, the multiple personalities of Elizabeth fight for control until she at last becomes well and discovers who she is, thereby making friends with the past. Eleanor's stay at Hill House involves the process of seeking her own identity and her desperate need to belong somewhere; and the narrative ends with her desire to join the spirits of the house. Mrs. Halloran in *The Sundial*, after playing foully for her supremacy in the household, seeks to establish herself as a queen. Her desire is to reign over the family, but each of the other characters strives to maintain his own dignity and pride. Merricat eliminates her family, outmaneuvers Charles, and becomes her sister's protectress before she feels secure and free to be herself, not realizing that they are now doomed.

As stated previously, the Jackson world is set apart from the usual world. In the psychological stories, the reader is carried through the convolutions of the protagonist's mind — a detour from normal everyday events. In *We Have Always Lived in the Castle*, the isolation is both physical and mental. The Blackwoods are isolated from the rest of the community, but Merricat with her psychotic nature is also isolated from the normal understanding of others. The remaining novels, too, involve groups that are outside the pale of ordinary living; for example, *The Road Through the Wall* has its own milieu in Pepper Street, which the reader sees, on the one hand, as typical, but, on the other, as the very special environment of a closed society. The would-be survivors in the Halloran mansion cling together as they prepare to live in the new world, since they alone seem to have been chosen to see it; and Dr. Montague's people, isolated in Hill House, experience contact with the spirit world.

Because few close, meaningful relationships exist among her fictional people, her characters experience no deep emotions except those of fear and anxiety; no strong love; no strong anger, jealousy, or hate. The most violent moments of hatred are found in *The Bird's Nest* when two of the multiple personalities of Elizabeth battle in one scene to dominate each other and in *We Have Always Lived in the Castle* in which Merricat has in the past hated her family and now vaguely (in a psychotic state) hates the villagers, who are on the periphery of the scene. She hates and fears Charles, but the moment that the object of her hatred is removed, she is in a euphoric state, knowing that she is safe, that no outside forces will take Constance away from her. Her relationship with Constance is closer than that of any other characters; and, because they feel secure in each other, Constance and Merricat are prepared to withstand the terrors of the outside world. The vague hatred that other characters feel appears often in the form of prejudice, like that of the villagers for the Blackwoods or of the Pepper Street families for the one Jewish family on the block. This hatred is a chronic illness in a society in which there is more hate than love.

Miss Jackson avoids ugliness or grisly realistic details of unpleasantness. When death occurs, which is seldom, it happens offstage as in *Road Through the Wall*, or is disposed of in a sentence or two as in *The Haunting of Hill House* when Eleanor crashes into the tree and as in *The Sundial* when Orianna Halloran is found lying at the bottom of the stairs. The body is carried off to rest beside the sundial on the lawn, but no unpleasant details are given. At the end of "The Lottery," the reader discovers with horror what is about to happen; but the story ends with the casting of the first stones. Miss Jackson prefers to leave the sordid details to the reader's imagination.

Again one notes that there is a lack of religion or of reference to

God in Miss Jackson's work: the characters struggle against
loneliness, insanity, or the hatred of others, but they never call upon
God for aid. God is nonexistent. Even in *The Sundial* the would-be
voyagers do not see or anticipate a supernatural being. Mrs.
Halloran is to be supreme ruler, and she does not intend to take
orders from anyone. Fanny's father acts as a comic-ominous being
who hovers about somewhere in space but has no specific authority.
Only the domain of spirits manifests itself in the presence of ghosts.
Beyond this manifestation, the hereafter is a big nothing, which, if
not polluted already, will soon be so by contact with humans.

Many of Miss Jackson's people, the villains, lack sensitivity and an
awareness of the needs of others; and, because of this lack, they in-
tentionally or unintentionally inflict pain. Since these people are not
grotesques but ordinary human beings, the discovery of evil beneath
the seeming good is especially terrifying, as in "The Lottery." The
outward grotesques are those characters who have ceased to function
normally, having been trapped in a world of shadows, such as Mrs.
Montague in "Island," or Elizabeth in *The Bird's Nest;* but they are
in most cases sympathetic if vulnerable persons.

Because Miss Jackson does not concentrate on love, on sexual
relationships, or on broad social problems, her fiction differs from
the popular, usual fictional fare of the day; nor does her work have
any kinship to the so-called modern Gothic novels. Instead, her
sphere is that of the individual involved in good and evil; therefore,
her work resembles more that of a modern Hawthorne or Edgar
Allan Poe. Her family tales, so different from the rest of her work,
revolve around the humor that arises from the problems of daily living; and they resemble other such family chronicles as Jean Kerr's
Please Don't Eat the Daisies or the stories of Betty MacDonald.

III *Achievement*

Delightful as Miss Jackson's humor is, and touches of it are found
throughout her fiction, it is not for the family chronicles that she will
be remembered although the story "Charles" has become a favorite
with anthologists. Her most effective tale is still "The Lottery"; but,
even if she had not written "The Lottery," she would still be an important writer. Her greatest strengths are in the expert handling of
humor, mystery, ambiguity, and suspense. Her wit and imagination
have created off-beat and original stories. Her characters are authentic, if often strange, people; and, as the critics point out, her prose
style is excellent. Why? Because her style is admirably suited to the

purposes of the storyteller: she does not write long, unwieldy sentences cluttered with abstract nouns or long metaphorical passages of description; her thoughts and sentiments are not muddied through endless philosophical meanderings; there is no attempt at affectation or fussiness. Instead, she chooses a simple, unadorned direct, clear manner of speaking to her reader. Her lines flow evenly, smoothly, and have a distinct rhythm. She shows a meticulousness in word choice and a deft manipulation of words; she has a poet's ear. She has, also, an excellent sense of timing with a punch line, but more often, her sense of fun creeps into the lines and takes the reader by surprise. Her wit and imagination add sparkle to her prose.

Miss Jackson is not, however, a major writer; and the reason she will not be considered one is that she saw herself primarily as an entertainer, as an expert storyteller and craftsman. She has insights to share with her readers; but her handling of the material — the surprise twists, the preoccupation with mystery and fantasy, her avoidance of strong passions, her versatility, and her sense of sheer fun — may not be the attributes of the more serious writer who wishes to come to grips with the strong passions of ordinary people in a workaday world, who prefers to deal directly with the essential problems of love, death, war, disease, poverty, and insanity in its most ugly aspects. Even with "The Lottery" one wonders if Miss Jackson may have chosen the situation for its shock value. The message is, nevertheless, effective; and the story is superb, regardless of the intent of the author. Despite the lack of critical attention, her books continue to be popular with those people who are sensitive, imaginative, and fun-loving; and perhaps, in the long run, that popularity will be what counts.

Notes and References

Preface
1. "School of One," *Newsweek*, LXVI (August 23, 1965), 83B.

Chapter One
1. Information in letter dated February 8, 1971, from Mrs. Leslie H. Jackson to the author.
2. *Ibid.*
3. Diary entry, June 30, 1933.
4. Diary entry, February 3, 1933.
5. Diary entry, December, 1932.
6. From letter of Professor H. W. Herrington to the author, June 1, 1971.
7. "Editorial," *Spectre*, Fall, 1939.
8. "Editorial," *Spectre*, Winter, 1940.
9. "Three Sonnets," *Spectre*, Winter, 1940, p. 16.
10. "Editorial," *Spectre*, Spring, 1940, p. 3.
11. "Editorial," *Spectre*, Summer, 1940, pp. 2 - 3.
12. Harvey Breit, "A Talk with Miss Jackson," *New York Times Book Review*, June 26, 1949, p. 15.
13. "Psychological Thriller," *Time magazine*, LVII (April 23, 1951), 114; Paul Pickrel, "Outstanding Novels," *Yale Review*, XL (Summer, 1951), 767.
14. Letter dated March 22, 1971, from Mr. Murry Karmiller to the author.
15. Letter dated June 25, 1971, from Mrs. June Mintz to the author.
16. Letter dated January 18, 1971, from Howard Nemerov to the author.
17. "Introduction," *Special Delivery* (Boston, 1960), p. 1.
18. "What I Want to Know Is, What Do Other People Cook With?" *Good Housekeeping*, CLIII (July, 1961), 14, 17.
19. Letter dated March 22, 1971, from Mr. Murry Karmiller to the author.
20. "Writing Alums Return," *Daily Orange*, April 28, 1965, p. 1.
21. *Ibid.*, p. 5.
22. "Poet Nemerov Appraises Shirley Jackson's Works," *Bennington Banner*, August 9, 1965, p. 10.
23. *Ibid.*
24. *Ibid.*

25. Letter dated March 18, 1971, from Mrs. Joanne Schnurer to the author.

26. Letter dated March 31, 1971, from Mrs. George W. Wheelwright III to the author.

27. Letter dated March 18, 1971, from Mrs. Joanne Schnurer to the author.

Chapter Two

1. "The Beautiful Stranger," *Come Along With Me* (New York, 1968), p. 64.

2. *Ibid.*, p. 72.

3. "Island," *Ibid.*, pp. 85 - 86.

4. *Ibid.*, p. 92.

5. "The Daemon Lover," *The Lottery, or The Adventures of James Harris* (New York, 1949), p. 8.

6. "The Visit," *Come Along With Me*, p. 98.

7. "The Renegade," *Harper's*, CXCVII (November, 1948), 48.

8. *Ibid.*, p. 49.

9. *Ibid.*, p. 50.

10. "After You, My Dear Alphonse," *The New Yorker*, XVIII (January 16, 1943), 52.

11. Sir James George Frazer, "The Scapegoat," *The Golden Bough* (New York: 1951), pp. 253 - 54.

12. "Biography of a Story," *Come Along With Me*, pp. 223 - 24.

13. Undated letter from Miss Jackson to her mother.

14. "Come Along With Me," *Come Along With Me*, p. 24.

15. "Island," *ibid.*, p. 95.

16. *Ibid.*, p. 92.

17. "The Visit," *ibid.*, p. 98.

18. "The Lottery," *ibid.*, p. 236.

Chapter Three

1. *The Road Through the Wall* (New York, 1969), pp. 7 - 8.

2. Robert Halsband, "Sidestreet, U.S.A.," *Saturday Review*, XXXI (February 28, 1948), 15.

Chapter Four

1. *Hangsaman* (New York, 1951), p. 121.

2. John O. Lyons, *The College Novel in America* (Carbondale, 1962), pp. 62 - 67.

3. Alice S. Morris, "Adventure into Reality," *New York Times Book Review*, April 22, 1951, p. 5.

4. W. T. Scott, "Dreaming Girl," *Saturday Review*, XXXIV (May 5, 1951), 11.

5. Paul Pickrel, "Outstanding Novels," *Yale Review*, XL (Summer, 1951), p. 767.

6. *The Bird's Nest, The Magic of Shirley Jackson* (New York, 1966), p. 199.

7. Dan Wickendan, "Shirley Jackson Once More Weaves Her Dramatic and Satiric Spell," *New York Herald Tribune Book Review*, June 20, 1954, p. 1.

8. William Peden, "Bedeviled Lady," *Saturday Review*, XXXVI (July 17, 1954), 11 - 12.

9. Edmund Fuller, review of *The Bird's Nest, Chicago Sunday Tribune*, June 27, 1954, p. 4.

10. Letter to her mother, Mrs. Leslie H. Jackson, dated June 12 (no year), probably 1956.

11. Letter to Miss Jackson's mother (no date), probably 1956. Film was released in 1956.

Chapter Five

1. *The Sundial* (New York, 1958), p. 39.

2. Edmund Fuller, review of *The Sundial, Chicago Sunday Tribune*, February 23, 1958, p. 13.

3. Harvey Swados, "What Is This World?" *The New Republic*, CXXXVIII (March 3, 1958), 19.

4. Peter Girven, "An Altogether Extraordinary Household," *New York Herald Tribune Book Review*, February 16, 1958, p. 5.

5. William Peden, "The 'Chosen Few,' " *Saturday Review*, XLI (March 8, 1958), 18.

6. Jean Holzhauer, "Interpretation," *Commonweal*, LXVIII (April 4, 1958), 20 - 21.

7. Norman Shrapnel, review of *The Sundial, Manchester (England) Guardian*, August 19, 1958, p. 2.

8. *The Haunting of Hill House* (New York, 1959), p. 211.

9. Warren Beck, review of *The Haunting of Hill House, Chicago Sunday Tribune*, October 18, 1959, p. 3.

10. Edmund Fuller, "Terror Lived There Too," *New York Times Book Review*, October 18, 1959, p. 4.

11. Maxwell Geismar, "Annals of Magic," *Saturday Review*, XLII (October 31, 1959), 19.

12. Undated letter from Shirley Jackson to her mother.

13. *We Have Always Lived in the Castle* (New York, 1962), p. 1.

14. Max Steele, "I Like the Death Cup Mushroom," *New York Herald Tribune*, September 23, 1962, p. 8.

15. "Nightshade Must Fall," *Time* magazine, September 21, 1962, p. 93.

16. Ihab Hassan, "Three Hermits on a Hill," *New York Times Book Review*, September 23, 1962, p. 5.

17. Louis Untermeyer, review of *We Have Always Lived in the Castle, New York Times Book Review*, September 23, 1962, p. 9.

18. Wilfrid Sheed, "The Stage," *Commonweal*, November 11, 1966, p. 167.

Chapter Six
1. *Life Among the Savages, The Magic of Shirley Jackson* (New York, 1966), pp. 385 - 86.
2. *Raising Demons, ibid.*, p. 548.

Chapter Seven
1. "Experience and Fiction," *Come Along With Me*, p. 208.

Selected Bibliography

PRIMARY SOURCES

1. Novels
The Road Through the Wall. New York: Farrar, Straus and Company, 1948.
Hangsaman. New York: Farrar, Straus and Company, 1951.
The Bird's Nest. New York: Farrar, Straus and Young, 1954.
The Sundial. New York: Farrar, Straus and Company, 1958.
The Haunting of Hill House. New York: Viking Press, 1959.
We Have Always Lived in the Castle. New York: Viking Press, 1962.
2. Fictionalized Autobiography
Life Among the Savages. New York: Farrar, Straus and Company, 1953.
Raising Demons. New York: Farrar, Straus and Company, 1957.
3. Children's Works
Witchcraft of Salem Village. New York: Random House, 1956.
The Bad Children (play). Chicago: The Dramatic Publishing Company, 1958.
Nine Magic Wishes. New York: The Crowell-Collier Press, 1963.
4. Short Story Collections
The Lottery, or The Adventures of James Harris. New York: Farrar, Straus and Company, 1949.
The Magic of Shirley Jackson. Ed. Stanley Edgar Hyman. New York: Farrar, Straus and Giroux, Inc., 1966.
Come Along With Me. Ed. Stanley Edgar Hyman. New York: The Viking Press, 1968.
5. Special Works
Special Delivery. Boston: Little, Brown and Company, 1960.
6. Articles
"Fame." *The Writer,* LXI (August, 1948), 265 - 66.
"Life Romantic." *Good Housekeeping,* CXXIX (December, 1949), 165 - 67.
"On Being a Faculty Wife." *Mademoiselle,* XLIV (December, 1956), 116 - 17.
"The Pleasures and Perils of Dining Out With Children." *McCall's,* LXXXIV (March, 1957), 54.

167

"How to Enjoy a Family Quarrel." *McCall's*, LXXXIV (September, 1957), 37.

"Mother, Honestly!" *Good Housekeeping*, CXLVII (September, 1959), 24.

"Karen's Complaint." *Good Housekeeping*, CXLIX (November, 1959), 38.

"The Lost Kingdom of Oz." *The Reporter*, XXI (December 10, 1959), 42 - 43.

"Comment" (upon the death of Leonard Brown [1904 - 1960]). *Syracusan 10*, II, 3 (March, 1960), 18.

"The Case for Dinner-Table Silence." *Good Housekeeping*, CL (March, 1960), 42.

"Out of the Mouths of Babes." *Good Housekeeping*, CLI (July, 1960), 36.

"Questions I Wish I'd Never Asked." *Good Housekeeping*, CLII (March, 1961), 50 ff.

"What I Want to Know Is, What Do Other People Cook With?" *Good Housekeeping*, CLIII (July, 1961), 14 ff.

"No, I Don't Want to Go to Europe." *Saturday Evening Post*, CCXXXVII, 22 (June 6, 1964), 8 - 10.

"Experience and Fiction." *The Writer*, 82, 1 (January, 1969), 9 - 14, 45. (Excerpted from *Come Along With Me*.)

7. Short Stories

"My Life With R. H. Macy." *New Republic*, CV (December 22, 1941), 862 ff.

"After You, My Dear Alphonse." *The New Yorker*, XVIII (January 16, 1943), 51 - 53.

"Come Dance With Me in Ireland." *The New Yorker*, XIX (May 15, 1943), 44 - 50.

"Afternoon in Linen." *The New Yorker*, XIX (September 4, 1943), 35, 38 - 39.

"On the House." *The New Yorker*, XIX (October 30, 1943), 77 - 79.

"A Fine Old Firm." *The New Yorker*, XX (March 4, 1944), 64 - 67.

"Villager." *American Mercury*, LIX (August, 1944), 186 - 90.

"Colloquy." *The New Yorker*," XX (August 5, 1944), 45.

"Little Old Lady." *Mademoiselle*, XXXIII (September, 1944), 243 - 45.

"Trial by Combat." *The New Yorker*, XX (December 16, 1944), 72, 74 - 76.

"When Things Get Dark." *The New Yorker*, XX (December 30, 1944), 40 - 43.

"A Cauliflower in Her Hair." *Mademoiselle*, XXXII (December, 1944), 102, 162.

"Behold the Child Among His Newborn Blisses." *Cross-Section*. Ed. E. Seaver. New York: L. B. Fischer, 1944, pp. 292 - 98.

"Whistler's Grandmother." *The New Yorker*, XXI (May 5, 1954), 59 - 61.

"It Isn't the Money I Mind." *The New Yorker*, XXI (August 25, 1945), 46, 48 - 49.

"Men with Their Big Shoes." Yale Review, XXXVI, 3 (March, 1947), 447 - 55.

"The Lottery." *The New Yorker*, XXIV (June 26, 1948), 25 - 28.

"Charles." *Mademoiselle*, XXXVI (July, 1948), 87, 114.

"Pillar of Salt." *Mademoiselle*, XXXVI (October, 1948), 152 - 53, 242 - 50.

"Renegade." *Harper's*, CXCVII (November, 1948), 37 - 43.

"The Tooth," *Hudson Review*, 4 (1948), 503 ff.

"Seven Types of Ambiguity." *Story*, XXXII (Fall, 1948), 242 - 50.

"Phantom Lover." *Woman's Home Companion*, LXXVI (February, 1949), 24 - 25.

"Third Baby's the Easiest." *Harper's*, CXCVIII (May, 1949), 58 - 63.

"Family Magician." *Woman's Home Companion*, LXXVI (September, 1949), 23, 92 - 93, 98, 100.

"Wishing Dime." *Good Housekeeping*, CXXIX (September, 1949), 34 - 35.

"My Son and the Bully." *Good Housekeeping*, CXXIX (October, 1949), 38.

"Lovely Night." *Collier's*, CXXV (April 8, 1950), 14 - 15.

"The Summer People." *Charm*, LXXIII, 1 (September, 1950), 108 - 109, 193 - 97.

"All the Girls Were Dancing." *Collier's*, CXXVI (November 11, 1950), 36.

"The Island." *New Mexico Quarterly Review*, XX, 3 (1950), 294 ff.

"Account Closed." *Good Housekeeping*, CXXX (April, 1950), 52 - 53.

"About Two Nice People." *Ladies' Home Journal*, LXVIII (July, 1951), 48 - 49.

"Mrs. Melville Makes A Purchase." *Charm*, LXXXV, 2 (October, 1951), 92, 114 - 19.

"Monday Morning." *Woman's Home Companion*, LXXVIII (November, 1951), 21.

"The Lovely House." *New World Writing*. Second Mentor Selection. New American Library of World Literature. New York: New American Library, 1952, pp. 130 - 50.

"Night We All Had Grippe." *Harper's*, CCIV (January, 1952), 74 - 78.

"Look Ma, We're Moving." *Good Housekeeping*, CXXXIV (February, 1952), 49.

"First Car Is the Hardest." *Harper's*, CCIV (February, 1952), 79 - 83.

"The House." *Woman's Day*, XV, 8 (May, 1952), 62 - 63, 115 - 19.

"Strangers." *Collier's*, CXXIX (May 10, 1952), 24 - 25.

"Most Wonderful Thing." *Good Housekeeping*, CXXXIV (June, 1952), 49.

"Nice Day for a Baby." *Woman's Home Companion*, LXXIX (July, 1952), 34 - 35.

"Journey with a Lady." *Harper's*, CCV (July, 1952), 75 - 81.

"Box." *Woman's Home Companion*, LXXIX (November, 1952), 25.

"Visions of Sugarplums." *Woman's Home Companion*, LXXIX (December, 1952), 42 - 43.

"Day of Glory." *Woman's Day*, XVI, 5 (February, 1953), 32, 87, 89.

"The Clothespin Dolls." *Woman's Day*, XVI, 6 (March, 1953), 36, 163 - 66.

"List Found in a Coat Pocket." *Vogue*, CXXI (April 15, 1953), 59.

"Worldly Goods." *Woman's Day*, XVI, 8 (May, 1953), 10 - 11, 178 - 79.

"Shopping Trip." *Woman's Home Companion*, LXXX (June, 1953), 40 - 41.

"The Second Mrs. Ellenoy." *Reader's Digest*, LXIII (July, 1953), 113 - 15.

"Lucky to Get Away." *Woman's Day*, XVI, 2 (August, 1953), 26, 117 - 19.

"An International Incident." *The New Yorker*, XXIX (September 12, 1953), 92, 95 - 96, 98 - 101.

"So Late on Sunday Morning." *Woman's Home Companion*, LXXX (September, 1953), 40, 47 - 48.

"Alone in a Den of Cubs." *Woman's Day*, XVII, 3 (December, 1953), 42 - 43, 107 - 08.

"Don't Tell Daddy." *Woman's Home Companion*, LXXXI (February, 1954), 42 - 43.

"Bulletin." *Fantasy and Science Fiction*, VI, 3 (March, 1954), 46.

"Aunt Gertrude." *Harper's*, CCVIII (April, 1954), 50 - 53.

"Mother Is a Fortune Hunter." *Woman's Home Companion*, LXXXI (May, 1954), 48.

"One Ordinary Day With Peanuts." *Fantasy and Science Fiction*, VIII (January, 1955), 53.

"Queen of the May." *McCall's*, LXXXII (April, 1955), 47.

"Little Magic." Woman's Home Companion, LXXXIII (January, 1956), 28 - 29.

"One Last Chance." *McCall's*, LXXXIII (April, 1956), 52 - 53.

"It's Only a Game." *Harper's*, CCXII (May, 1956), 36 - 39.

"The Sneaker Crisis." *Woman's Day*, XX (September, 1956), 29, 101 - 02.

"Every Boy Should Learn to Play the Trumpet." *Woman's Home Companion*, LXXXIII (October, 1956), 36 - 37.

"The Omen." *Fantasy and Science Fiction*, XIV, 3 (March, 1958), 118.

"Stranger in Town." *Saturday Evening Post*, CCXXXI, 48 (May 30, 1959), 18 - 19.

"Santa Claus, I Love You." *Good Housekeeping*, CXLIX (December, 1959), 38.

"A Great Voice Stilled." *Playboy*, VII, 3 (March, 1960), 57 - 58, 91.

"Louisa, Please." *Ladies' Home Journal*, LXXVII (May, 1960), 48 - 49.

"All She Said Was Yes." *Vogue*, CXL (November 1, 1962), 142 - 43 ff.

"Birthday Party." *Vogue*, CXLI (January 1, 1963), 118 ff. Reprinted in *The Best American Short Stories, 1964*. Ed. Martha Foley and David Burnett. Boston: Houghton Mifflin, 1964.

"The Bus." *Saturday Evening Post*, CCXXXVIII, 6 (March 27, 1965), 62 - 67.

"Home." *Ladies' Home Journal*, LXXXII, 8 (August, 1965), 64, 116 - 118.

"The Possibility of Evil." *Saturday Evening Post*, CCXXXVIII, 25 (December 18, 1965), 61 - 69.

SECONDARY SOURCES

Very little has been written about Shirley Jackson; in fact, in the sources listed, comments are often limited to a sentence or two. None of the works, therefore, is very helpful in interpreting or understanding her. Some of the reviews are useful, and, if so, are mentioned in the text. Those included here are representative.

1. Bibliography

PHILLIPS, ROBERT S. "Shirley Jackson: A Checklist." *Bibliographical Society of America Papers*, LVI, 1 (January, 1962), 110 - 13. Very helpful. Prepared with the help of Miss Jackson.

———. "Shirley Jackson: A Chronology and a Supplementary Checklist." *Bibliographical Society of America Papers*, LX, 1 (April, 1966), 203 - 13. Chronology had been approved by Miss Jackson before her death. Brings the bibliography up to date as of 1965. Rather complete.

2. Biography

ANON. "Writing Alums Return." *Syracuse University Daily Orange*, April 12, 1965, p. 1. Describes the on-campus activities of Mr. Hyman and Miss Jackson on their first trip back to Syracuse.

———. *New York World-Telegram and Sun*, August 9, 1965, p. 17. Obituary.

———. *New York Times*, August 10, 1965, p. 29. Obituary. Little biographical information, but a useful resumé of previous interviews with Miss Jackson; helpful in matters of subject and style. States: ". . . she wrote with remarkable tautness and economy of style, and her choice of words and phrases was unerring in building a story's mood."

———. "School of One." *Newsweek*, August 23, 1965, p. 83B. Obituary. Mentioned in preface of this work. Declares Shirley Jackson an absolute original. The most meaningful of the general reviews.

———. *Publisher's Weekly*, CLXXXVIII (August 23, 1965), 70. Obituary. Acknowledges Miss Jackson's commercial and critical success and her artistry. Otherwise, rather superficial.

BREIT, HARVEY. "Talk with Miss Jackson." *New York Times*, June 26, 1949, p. 15. Discussed in the text. Miss Jackson gives her views on writing, her literary likes and dislikes. An early interview after publication of the collection *The Lottery*.

CICCOLELLA, CATHY. "Jackson Credits SU with Writing Start." *Syracuse University Daily Orange*, April 28, 1965, p. 1. An interview with Miss Jackson on her last visit to Syracuse.

EDGE, P. *Wilson Library Bulletin*, XXXVIII (December, 1963), 352. Brief review mentioning Miss Jackson's first novel and one or two other works with the purpose of commenting on the latest children's book *Nine Magic Wishes*.

HYMAN, STANLEY EDGAR. "Shirley Jackson, 1919 - 1965." *Saturday Evening Post*, CCXXXVIII, 25 (December 18, 1965), 61 - 69. Sensitive memorial to his wife; excellent portrait of her as a human being and as a writer.

KREBS, ALBIN. " 'The Lottery' Brought Fame." *New York Herald Tribune*, August 10, 1965. Obituary.

KUNITZ, STANLEY J. "Shirley Jackson." *Twentieth Century Authors*. First Supplement. New York: Wilson, 1955, 483. Scanty biographical information. Not very helpful.

NICHOLS, LEWIS. "Demonologist." *New York Times Book Review*, October 7, 1962, p. 8. Written after Miss Jackson visited New York for ceremonies attending publication of *We Have Always Lived in the Castle*. Mentions her collection on demonology but stresses family interests.

NYREN, DOROTHY. *A Library of Literary Criticism*. New York: F. Ungar Publishing Company, 1960. Pp. 246 - 48. Excerpts from early reviews, five from 1949 dealing with the short stories; one dealing with *Hangsaman;* another with *The Bird's Nest*. All reviews favorable except that of Donald Barr, *New York Times*, who complains that "the middle class emotion of embarrassment has been substituted for many of the human passions."

PHILLIPS, ROBERT S. "The *Spectre* of Shirley Jackson: A Short History of a Literary Phenomenon at Syracuse." *Syracuse 10*, III, 3 (March, 1961), 11 - 12, 28 - 29. Interesting account of Miss Jackson's undergraduate years with emphasis on the history of the literary magazine founded by her and Mr. Hyman.

WARFEL, HARRY R. *American Novelists of Today*. New York: American Book Company, 1951. P. 227. Short biographical sketch mentions only her first novel and *The Lottery* collection.

3. Critical Discussions

ALDRIDGE, JOHN W. *After the Lost Generation: A Critical Study of the Writers of Two Wars*. New York: McGraw-Hill Book Company, Inc., 1958. Pp. 146, 195, 197. Cites Shirley Jackson as one of the prose purists who turned from a world of social manners to the creation of private worlds. In this category also are Paul Bowles, Truman Capote, and Frederick Buechner.

BROOKS, CLEANTH, and ROBERT PENN WARREN. "Interpretation." *Understanding Fiction*. Second Edition. New York: Appleton-Century-Crofts, 1959. Pp. 72 - 76. Examines "The Lottery" as normal piece of fiction leaning toward the fable and the parable forms and exposing the doubleness of the human spirit: good-humoredness and cruelty.

EISINGER, CHESTER E. *Fiction of the Forties*. Chicago: University of Chicago Press, 1963. Pp. 288 - 89. Says Miss Jackson "manages a low-keyed and quiet nihilism" and assumes the presence of evil everywhere; also that her pessimistic view of experience is occasionally "obscured by the manipulation of her paradoxes."

ELLIOT, GEORGE P. "The Truth about Fiction." *Holiday*, XXXIX, 3 (March, 1966), 110. Speaks optimistically of current fiction, especially the variety found in the short story form. Finds fantasies particularly congenial to ideas; "The Lottery" celebrated not only for author's skill in surprising the reader but for the story idea. The scapegoats were not only for primitives. We have scapegoats too.

FIEDLER, LESLIE A. *Love and Death in the American Novel*. New York: Criterion Books, 1960. P. 469. Discusses the evasive symbolism of Isaac Rosenfeld and Paul Goodman and their Kafkaesque tendencies, at the same time deploring "The Lottery" as an "unwitting travesty" of their American adaptation of Kafka; calling it a "standard middlebrow anthology piece."

HEILMAN, ROBERT B. *Modern Short Stories*. New York: Harcourt, Brace and Company, 1950. Pp. 384 - 85. Discussion of "The Lottery." Helpful interpretation; but concentrates on the shock ending, which is not realistic. Says that author should have made clear her symbolic intention earlier in the story.

HYMAN, STANLEY EDGAR. *The Promised End*. New York: World Publishing Company, 1963. Pp. 264, 349, 365. Discussion of the James Harris ("The Daemon Lover") ballads; of ceremonial initiations leading to maturity as in *Hangsaman;* also compares Mrs. Halloran's donning of golden crown to Agamemnon's incurring the wrath of the gods and his own death by treading on the carpet of royal purple. Otherwise, does not discuss Miss Jackson's works.

LAINOFF, SEYMOUR. "Jackson's 'The Lottery,' " *The Explicator*, XII (March, 1954), item 34. Acknowledges Miss Jackson's debt to Frazer's *Golden Bough* as a modern representation of the scapegoat rite. Emphasizes rite's purpose and the fact that beneath our civilized surface there are still patterns of savage behavior. But says that the author is optimistic, for some villages have abandoned the lottery.

LYONS, JOHN O. *The College Novel in America*, Carbondale: Southern Illinois University Press, 1962. Pp. 62 - 67, 100, 158, 186. Discusses *Hangsaman* as a representative college novel and not as a portrait of a schizophrenic girl. Interprets Natalie's other self (Tony) as another college student, a Lesbian.

WEST, RAY B., JR. *The Short Story in America*. Chicago: Henry Regnery Company, 1952. Pp. 115 - 16. In discussing the writers of the 1940's, says a few writers veer in the direction of the symbol for its own sake. Names Shirley Jackson among them as using a "brittle and abstract, but 'rigged' symbolism."

4. Book Reviews (Selected)

a. *The Road Through the Wall* (1948)

ANON. *The New Yorker*, XXIII (February 21, 1948), 94, 97. Says the story comes off very well although suburban life has been treated exhaustively in the fiction of the past twenty years; also that most of its success derives from the author's style.

HALSBAND, ROBERT. "Sidestreet, U.S.A." *Saturday Review*, XXXI (February 28, 1948), 14 - 15. Says Miss Jackson's talent is a considerable one: "She fits together her jigsaw plot adroitly, and underlines every gesture and phrase with significance;" finds the characters highly original and depicted with an impersonal sympathy that is "reminiscent of Steinbeck at his best." Remarks on the clean simplicity of her style. Aside from the minor flaw of the populous cast, the story is good, he says. The best of the reviews.

McKay, Mildred Peterson. *Library Journal*, LXXIII (January 15, 1948), 123. One-paragraph synopsis with the comment that *Road* is a good story, well written.

Parke, Andrea. "Pepper Street." *New York Times Book Review*, February 22, 1948, p. 26. Favorable review commenting on the family relationships depicted with precision and subtle understanding; but finds Tod's suicide the one false note "in a book that otherwise has been written with an unerring sense of values."

b. *The Lottery* (Collection, 1949)

Anon. "Come On, Everyone." *Time*, LIII (May 23, 1949), 105 - 06. Generally favorable review.

Barr, Donald. "A Talent for Irony." *New York Times Book Review*, April 17, 1949, p. 4. At the same time that he praises Miss Jackson for her talent for irony, he criticizes the easy, economical style and unobtrusive dialogue that have become standard requirements for upper-middle-class magazine stories. Also says that a helplessness runs through all the stories and a substitution of the emotion of embarrassment for many of the other human emotions. Ends by calling this one of the most interesting books of short stories we have had in some time.

Farrelly, John. "Fiction Parade." *New Republic*, CXX (May 9, 1949), 26. Says one remembers more the disenchantment, loneliness, perilous confusion rather than any one particular piece of fiction from the collection.

Hilton, James. *New York Herald Tribune Book Review*, May 1, 1949, p. 4. Finds that these moving stories remind one of the elemental terrors of childhood. States that the whole collection will enhance Miss Jackson's reputation as a writer not quite like any other of her generation; says she sees life in her own style as Dali paints it; that her technique is sound.

c. *Hangsman* (1951)

Anon. "Psychological Thriller." *Time*, LVII (April 23, 1951), 114. Calls this "a description, simple and terrifying, of a young girl sinking into schizophrenia." Favorable review but considers the ending anticlimactic; however, says it proves that Miss Jackson can maintain the same eerie pressure (as the psychological chillers) at novel length.

Bullock, Florence H. *New York Herald Tribune Book Review*, April 22, 1951, p. 7. Praises *Hangsaman* as good fiction and (psychologically speaking) as good fact. Says "Miss Jackson writes with grace and precision of this tenuous borderline country of the emotionally disturbed."

MORRIS, ALICE S. "Adventure into Reality." *New York Times Book Review*, April 22, 1951, p. 5. Favorable but puzzling review. Calls this a work of artistic maturity and says there is no false note, but does not discuss the ending of the book. Interprets Tony as being a real person.

PICKREL, PAUL. "Outstanding Novels" *Yale Review*, XL (Summer, 1951), 767. Comments focus on the first half of the novel; says little or nothing about the last half; calls work an "extraordinarily perceptive picture of adolescence."

SCOTT, W. T. "Dreaming Girl." *Saturday Review*, XXXIV (May 5, 1951), 11. Feels that here the method of proceeding from realism to symbolic drama (which succeeded in "The Lottery") fails, and the structure of the novel falls apart; for the reader is not prepared for the schizoid fantasies. Just criticism and a good review.

STRONG, L. A. *The Spectator*, CLXXXVII (October 5, 1951), 452. Gives positive and negative comments. Says *Hangsaman* does not measure up to "The Lottery," but that "it confirms the belief that Miss Jackson is an exceptional writer." Believes she loses tension in the longer form.

d. *Life Among the Savages* (1953)

ANON. *The New Yorker*, XXIX (June 20, 1953), 101. Remarks that Miss Jackson has a true ear for the way children talk; then says, reservedly, "she writes of her household with a sort of nervous and observant detachment that is sometimes quite funny."

BENCHLEY, NATHANIEL. *New York Herald Tribune Book Review*, June 28, 1953, p. 1. Favorable review. Appreciates the humor.

COBB, JANE. *New York Times*, June 21, 1953, p. 6. Favorable review.

FULLER, EDMUND. *Chicago Sunday Tribune*, July 5, 1953, p. 3. Observes that Shirley Jackson has pinned down the contemporary, middle-class intellectual couple with young children definitively — the happenings, the sayings, the crises. Says it is not one of these cocksure chronicles.

LONG, MARGARET. *Saturday Review*, XXXVI (June 27, 1953), 36. Favorable.

STOER, M. W. *Christian Science Monitor*, July 9, 1953, p. 7. Positive comments, noting the studies of amiable despair that parents will recognize as typical. Appreciates also the solid foundations of affectionate family relationships underlying all, giving the book a wholesome aspect "that is altogether welcome."

e. *The Bird's Nest* (1954)

ANON. *The New Yorker*, XXX (June 26, 1954), 90. Praises style. Not very helpful.

———. "Strange Case of Miss R." *Time*, LXVI (June 21, 1954), 108. Rather superficial negative review. Indicates that work marks only scattered returns to her best form.

FULLER, EDMUND. *Chicago Sunday Tribune*, (June 27, 1954), p. 4. Positive. Considers this best novel: brilliant, swift, funny, frightening. "Her portrayal of a personality in disintegration is masterful." A negative factor, but apparently a minor one, in his estimation, is the too-easy resolution.

PEDEN, WILLIAM. "Bedeviled Lady." *Saturday Review*, XXXVI (July 17, 1954), 11 - 12. Another favorable review. Thinks Miss Jackson's reputation as a master of shock, surprise, and suspense is well-deserved. Points out her successful use of a variety of points of view. Indicates that she has done much more than "produce just another perceptive clinical study of emotional deterioration. She has created a kind of twentieth-century morality play." Mr. Peden includes other helpful and enlightening comments. Probably the best review of *The Bird's Nest*.

SCOTT, EVELYN. *New York Times*, June 20, 1954, p. 13. Acknowledges Miss Jackson's skill in detailing adolescent and childhood experiences but finds the book esthetically confusing.

WICKENDEN, DAN. *New York Herald Tribune Book Review*, June 20, 1954, p. 1. Favorable review; calls the book superlative entertainment and the best book Shirley Jackson has written; says the climax and its conclusions are "curiously moving."

f. *Raising Demons* (1957)

JONES, J. C. "Writer as Mother." *Saturday Review*, XL (January 19, 1957), 45. The most meaningful of these reviews. Indicates that this fresh, beguiling family chronicle is often a "shrewd and witty social document as well." Finds the baby "Mr. Beekman" one of the most engaging two-year-olds ever set down on paper, a tribute to Miss Jackson's skill with dialogue.

Other reviews tend to be favorable but show less enthusiasm than for *Life Among the Savages*.

g. *The Sundial* (1958)

ANON. *Times* (London) *Literary Supplement*, September 19, 1958, p. 534. Lukewarm review. Says readers will enjoy it, but finds the resulting concoction odd. Typical of several of the critical accounts.

GIRVIN, PETER. *New York Herald Tribune Book Review*, February 16, 1958, p. 5. Favorable review, but the critic admits (as do several others) that he is not sure of what Miss Jackson is up to; is this a spoof, a fantasy, a satire? Difficult to tell.

HOLZHAUER, JEAN. "Interpretation." *Commonweal*, LXVIII (April 4, 1958), 20 - 21. Suggests that the book may be an allegory and possibly anti-Catholic; even so, declares the story uneven.

MORRIS, A. S. *New York Times*, February 23, 1958, p. 5. Negative review; not very helpful. Finds work a waste of Miss Jackson's talents.

PEDEN, William. "The 'Chosen Few.'" *Saturday Review*, XLI (March 8, 1958), 18. Looks at the book as an ironic inquiry into the idiocy of mankind. There are startling incidents and unusual characters; he notes Miss Jackson's preoccupation with symbols. Good review.

SWADOS, HARVEY. "What Is This World?" *New Republic*, CXXXVIII

(March 3, 1958), 19. Makes the judgment that the book leaves a small impression due perhaps to Miss Jackson's calculated, carefully expressed contempt for mankind.

h. *The Haunting of Hill House* (1959)

ANON. *The New Yorker*, October 24, 1959, p. 197. Praises Miss Jackson's handling of her subject with effective vivid descriptions, but deplores the introduction of Mrs. Montague and her friend Arthur, who introduce a false note; the ending, then, he feels is melodramatic.

————. *Times* (London) *Literary Supplement*, September 16, 1960, p. 597. A positive review. Says that this is not a stock ghost story with stock characters, but a novel of "distinctiveness and genuine power."

BECKET, ROGER. *New York Herald Tribune Book Review*, October 25, 1959, p. 14. The most significant and perceptive of these reviews. Admits it is a good horror story but is essentially "a pathetic portrait of a needful creature on the edge of the unknown, crying out to belong and be loved."

GEISMAR, MAXWELL. "Annals of Magic." *Saturday Review*, XLII (October 31, 1959), 19, 31. Says Miss Jackson may be good at describing the problems of human pathology but is weak in describing the normal world of human relations. Objects to the supposedly sophisticated, but really embarrassing, relationship between Eleanor and Theodora. Also would like some explanation of the supernatural occurrences.

i. *We Have Always Lived in the Castle* (1962)

The reviews were almost unanimously favorable, and the following are representative.

GOODHEART, EUGENE. "O to be a Werewolf." *Saturday Review*, XLV (November 3, 1962), 47. Charm and comedy are stronger than the horror: "One might say that Miss Jackson has caught the comedy of the demonic, has spoofed the fantastic world as well as the real one."

HASSEN, IHAB. "Three Hermits on a Hill." *New York Times Book Review*, September 23, 1962, p. 5. Has always felt that "some writers should be read and never reviewed. Their talent is haunting and utterly oblique; their mastery of craft seems complete." Says that Miss Jackson is one of that group. All he can do is offer praise. Says she is a meticulous storyteller.

PRESCOTT, ORVILLE. *New York Times*, October 5, 1962, p. 31. Quotes the first paragraph of the novel, then says that she is the only woman alive who could have written that. Calls Miss Jackson a "literary sorceress of uncanny prowess." States that she has always been an original; as a storyteller she is expert, "deft in suggesting emotional atmosphere and adroit in conveying nuances of feeling." Her characters, though bizarre, are convincing.

Index

(The works of Shirley Jackson are listed under her name)

Aiken, Conrad, 38 - 39
Anderson, Marian, 24
Arents Pioneer Medal, 26
Austin, Jane, 102
Ayling, Dorothy, 18, 38

Beck, Warren, 133
Belitt, Ben, 35
Benchley, Robert, 36
Bennington Banner, 40, 41
Bennington College, 27, 31, 32, 34, 35
Blake, William, 21
Blondell, Joan, 103
Bloom, Claire, 122
Borden, Lizzie, 144
Bowen, Elizabeth, 29
Brand's *Popular Antiquities*, 21
Brandt, Carol, 68
Breadloaf Writers' Conference, 30, 39
Breit, Harvey, 28, 86
Brown, Leonard (Professor), 22, 23, 35
Bugbee, Clifford (Uncle), 17
Bugbee, Geraldine (Mrs. Leslie Jackson: mother), 17, 121, 135
Bugbee, John S. (Great-grandfather), 17, 121
Bugbee, Maxwell (Grandfather), 17
Bugbee, Samuel (Great-great-grandfather), 17
Bullock, Florence Haxton, 90
Burke, Kenneth, 35
Burlingame, California (site of *Road Through the Wall*), 18, 61, 78
Burney, Fanny, 29, 102

Capote, Truman, 68
Cerf, Bennet, 33
Chase, Mary Ellen, 30, 31
Chekhov, Anton, 41
Chute, B. J., 36
Ciardi, John, 38
Collier, John, 68
Cummington Fiction Conference, 30

Dahl, Roald, 122
Daily Orange, 39
Dali, Salvadore, 68
Defoe, Daniel: *Robinson Crusoe*, 109
Dinesen, Isak, 143
Duffield, Brainerd, 31

Ellison, Ralph, 35

Field, Evangeline (Grandmother), 17
Foster, Mrs. Thomas H., 28
Fraser, Sir James: *The Golden Bough*, 21
Fuller, Edmund, 102, 118, 134

Geismer, Maxwell, 134
Girven, Peter, 119
Glanvil, Joseph: *Sadducismus Triumphatus*, 67
Graves, Robert, 38
Greene, Anna Maxwell (Great-grandmother), 17

Halsband, Robert, 85
Harris, Julie, 122

179

Harrison, Benjamin, 17
Hassan, Ihab, 143
Hawthorne, Nathaniel, 52, 160; *Scarlet Letter*, 81
Herrington, H. W. (Professor), 20
Hilton, James, 68
Holzhauer, Jean, 120
Hopkins, Gerard Manley, 25
Hyman, Barry (Son), 31, 146, *149 - 53*
Hyman, (Schnurer), Joanne (Daughter), 27, 34, 35, 41, 42, 146, *149 - 53*
Hyman, Laurence (Son), 26, 69, 146, *149 - 54*
Hyman, Sarah (Daughter), 27, 34, 35, 40, 146, *149 - 53*, 156
Hyman, Stanley Edgar, 21, 25, 26, 27, 29, 30, 31, 32, 33, 35, 36, 38, 39, 40, 42, 43, 68, 69, 78, 103, 104, 135, *146 - 54*; *The Armed Vision*, 27, 78 *The Promised End*, 39 "Talk of the Town," 32

Jackson, Barry (Brother), 18
Jackson, (Bugbee) Geraldine (Mother), 17, 121, 135
Jackson, Helen Hunt, 32
Jackson, Leslie (Father), 17, 18, 19
Jackson, Shirley: birth and family, 17; early years, 18 - 20; college years, 20 - 26; marriage and beginning of writing career, 26; move to Vermont 27; *New York Times* interview, 28 - 29; move to Westport, Conn., 30; back to North Bennington, 30; interview at Smith College, 30; faculty wife, 31 - 32; interest in the occult, 33 - 34; other activities of later years (1956 - 1965), 34 - 41; death, 40; Joanne's memories of her mother, 41 - 43; memorial by Howard Nemerov, 41
WORKS: ARTICLES
    "Experience and Fiction," 155
    "No, I Don't Want to Go to Europe," 37
    "What I Want to Know Is, What Do Other People Cook With?" 37
WORKS: FAMILY BOOKS
    Life Among the Savages, 27, 31, 34, 68, 69, *145 - 50*, 154

Raising Demons, 31, 34, 68, 69, 145, *150 - 54*
WORKS: OTHER NON-FICTION PROSE
    "Biography of a Story," 156
    "Notes for a Young Writer," 156
    Special Delivery, 36
    Witchcraft of Salem Village, 33 - 34
WORKS: NOVELS
    Bird's Nest, The, 32, 38, 68, *95 - 103*, 120, 123, 145, 157, 158, 159, 160; *Lizzie* (movie version), 32, 103
    Come Along With Me (unfinished novel), 39 - 40, 70; *Come Along Me* (anthology), 68, 155
    Hangsaman, 30, 32, 50, *86 - 95*, 101, 102, 120, 125, 145, 157, 158
    Haunting of Hill House, The, 23, 35, 38, 50, 104, *121 - 135*, 155, 156, 157, 158, 159; *Haunting, The* (movie version), 35, 105, 122
    Road Through the Wall, The, 18, 27, 76, *78 - 85*, 94, 102
    Sundial, The, 34, 75, 76, *104 - 121*, 125, 133, 140, 142, 144, 158, 159, 160
    We Have Always Lived in the Castle, 37, 38, 76, 104, 133, *135 - 44*, 158, 159; (play), 38, 144
WORKS: PLAYS
    Bad Children, The, 34
WORKS: POETRY
    "Pine Tree, The," 18
WORKS: SHORT STORIES
    "After You, My Dear Alphonse," 26, 61 - 62, 70
    "All She Said Was Yes," 59, 76
    "Aunt Gertrude," 150
    "Beautiful Stranger, The," *45 - 47*, 76, 157
    "Box, The," 69, 145
    "Bus, The," *53 - 54*, 72
    "Charles," 27, 30, 67, 69, 70, 72, 145, *146 - 47*, 160
    "Clothespin Dolls, The," 150
    "Come Dance With Me in Ireland," 26, 67
    "Daemon Lover, The," 50, 67, 73
    "Don't Tell Daddy," 150
    "Dorothy and My Grandmother and the Sailors," 67
    "Elizabeth," 62, 63, 67

"Every Boy Should Learn to Play the Trumpet," 150
"Family Magician," 150
"Fine Old Firm, A," 61
"First Car Is the Hardest," 145
"Flower Garden," 67, 74, 75, 76
"Home," 53, 73, 155
"I Know Who I Love," 62
"International Incident," 150
"Island, The," *47 - 49*, 70, 71, 75, 160
"It's Only A Game," 150
"Janice," (first short story), 21
"Little House, The," 55, 56 - 57, 73, 76
"List Found in a Coat Pocket," 145
"Lottery, The," 21, 24, 27, 28, 31, 33, 39, 44, *63 - 67*, 68, 70, 71, 72, 74, 76, 78, 106, 133, 141, 156, 157, 159, 160, 161

Lottery, or the Adventures of James Harris, The (anthology of short stories), 28, 67
"Lucky to Get Away," 150

Magic of Shirley Jackson (anthology of short stories along *The Bird's Nest, Life Among the Savages,* and *Raising Demons*), 68
"Monday Morning," 145
"My Life With R. H. Macy," 26
"My Son and the Bully," 69, 145
"Night We All Had Grippe, The," 69, 145, 149
Nine Magic Wishes (children's picture book), 38
"On the House," 58 - 59, 72
"One Ordinary Day with Peanuts," 33, 59, 70, 72
"Phantom Lover," (See "The Daemon Lover"), *50 - 51*
"Pillar of Salt," 27, 67
"Possibility of Evil," *57 - 58*, 72
"Renegade, The," 27, *60 - 61*, 67, 155, 157, 158, 159
"Rock, The," 53, 74 - 75, 155
"Seven Types of Ambiguity," 27, 59, 67, 76
"Shopping Trip," 69, 145
"Sneaker Crisis, The," 150
"So Late on Sunday Morning," 150

"Summer People," *55 - 56*, 73, 155
"Third Baby Is the Easiest, The," 69, 145
"Tooth, The," 27, 49, 53, 67
"Trial by Combat," 57, 72
"Villager, The," *62 - 63*, 67
"Visions of Sugar Plums," 145
"Visit, The," 52, 71, 72, *73 - 74*, 75
"Whistler's Grandmother," 57, 72
"Worldly Goods," 150
James, Henry: *The Turn of the Screw*, 134
Johnson, A. E. (poet), 21, 25

Karmiller, Murray and Barbara, 31, 38
Kerr, Jean: *Please Don't Eat the Daisies*, 160

Library of Congress (Shirley Jackson manuscripts), 32
Lyons, John O.: *The College Novel in America.* 89

MacDonald, Betty, 160
McGinley, Phyllis, 38
Malamud, Bernard, 35
Metro-Goldwyn Mayer, 103
Miller, Arthur, 38
Mirken, June, 21, 25, 33
Morris, Alice S., 90

NAACP, 25
Nash, Ogden, 36
Nemerov, Howard, 33, 35, 36, 41, 117

O'Connor, Flannery, 77, 104; "A Good Man Is Hard to Find," 77; "Greenleaf," 77

Peden, William, 102, 119, 120
Pickrel, Paul, 94
Plantagenet, Richard, 136, 137
Poe, Edgar Allan: "Ligeia," 134, 160
Poltergeists, 123, 128
Pope, Alexander, 105
Porter, Katherine Anne, 29
Prince, Dr. Morton: *The Dissociation of a Personality*, 95

Richardson, Samuel: *Pamela*, 29, 123; Clarissa, 123; *Sir Charles Grandison*, 123
Ross, Harold, 64
Roughead, William, 134

Saki, 68
Saroyan, William, 39
Scott, W. T., 90
Sheed, Wilfrid, 144
Shrapnel, Norman, 120
Skinner, Cornelia Otis, 36
Spectre, The, (literary magazine), 21 - 25, 32
Stebbin, Reverend, 17
Steele, Max, 141
Swados, Harvey, 119
Syracusan, The (humor magazine), 21

Syracuse University, *20 - 26*, 32, 35, 39, 61

Thackeray, William Makepeace, 97
Thomas, Norman, 24
Thompson, Dorothy, 24
Twain, Mark, 36, 150

Untermeyer, Louis, 143

Violett, Ellen, 31

Walpole, Horace: *The Castle of Otranto*, 105, 107
Wickendan, Dan, 102
Williams, Emlyn, 122
Wise, Robert, 122
Wohnus, Peg, 34